Earn
what you're
worth

Earn

what you're

worth

Nicole Williams

with Cheri Hanson

A Perigee Book

Published by the Penguin Group
Penguin Group (USA) Inc.
375 Hudson Street, New York, New York 10014, USA
Penguin Group (Canada), 10 Alcorn Avenue, Toronto, Ontario M4V 3B2, Canada
(a division of Pearson Penguin Canada Inc.)
Penguin Books Ltd., 80 Strand, London WC2R 0RL, England
Penguin Group Ireland, 25 St. Stephen's Green, Dublin 2, Ireland (a division of Penguin Books Ltd.)
Penguin Group (Australia), 250 Camberwell Road, Camberwell, Victoria 3124, Australia
(a division of Pearson Australia Group Pty. Ltd.)
Penguin Books India Pvt. Ltd., 11 Community Centre, Panchsheel Park, New Delhi—110 017, India
Penguin Group (NZ), Cnr. Airborne and Rosedale Roads, Albany, Auckland 1310, New Zealand
(a division of Pearson New Zealand Ltd.)
Penguin Books (South Africa) (Pty.) Ltd., 24 Sturdee Avenue, Rosebank, Johannesburg 2196, South
Africa

Penguin Books Ltd., Registered Offices: 80 Strand, London WC2R 0RL, England

Copyright © 2005 by Nicole Williams
Text design by Tiffany Estreicher
Cover design by Liz Sheehan
Cover photos © by Lindsey Sui

PRINTING HISTORY
Perigee trade paperback edition / January 2005

PERIGEE is a registered trademark of Penguin Group (USA) Inc.
The "P" design is a trademark belonging to Penguin Group (USA) Inc.

ISBN: 0-399-53063-0

Library of Congress Cataloging-in-Publication Data
Williams, Nicole, 1970–
    Earn what you're worth / Nicole Williams.—1st Perigee paperback ed.
        p. cm.
    ISBN 0-399-53063-0
    1. Women—Salaries, etc. 2. Wealth—Psychological aspects. 3. Achievement motivation
in women. 4. Success—Psychological aspects. 5. Businesswomen—United
States—Interviews. 6. Women in the professions—United States—Interviews.   I. Title.

HD6061.W57 2005
650.1'2'082—dc22   2004053362

PRINTED IN THE UNITED STATES OF AMERICA

10   9   8   7   6   5   4   3   2   1

Because of Jennifer Wolfe Hannay

Table of Contents

Acknowledgments

One of the most important aspects of actually being and living what you're worth is asking for and accepting help. And let me tell you, this book is the culmination of the most heartfelt, brilliant, and passionate help around. I'm all about debt and my indebtedness goes out to:

My writing partner Cheri Hanson, the most thoughtful, actually full-of-thought woman I know. As sometimes frightening as it is, for getting into my head and capturing my stories, thoughts, and essence in writing. Edna (Roxy) Zurbuchen—"for her enormous capacity work" and more importantly her enormous capacity for caring for her Wildly Sophisticated family. Jennifer Wolfe Hannay, my soul sister and partner in business and in life.

For my agent, Kim Goldstein, for her continued belief, encouragement and for bringing her mom. For the team at Penguin. My editor, Michelle Howry, for her tremendous talent, inspiring discipline, and for a great title! To John Duff for driving me to want this as much for him, as for me. Liz Perl and Craig Burke for keeping the fire alive. Linda Lipman for her investment, vision, and partnership in Wildly Sophisticated.

For the team at Wildly Sophisticated Television: John Ritchie, Gillian Lowry, Rob Bromley, Sue Rideout, Thomas Hunt, and most especially to

Maureen Palmer for sharing her wine, insight, support, and for sticking it out to protect my vision.

For my business partners, Praveen Varshney and Paul Grehan, for enthusiastically sharing their insight, their own money, time, and most especially for cheering me on in most uncharacteristic of "accounting-like" ways! Con Buckley for being the most loyal and faithful friend and advisor. The team at VanCity Capital: Lee Davis, Robert Napoli, and Kristi Miller for being a "chick with balls."

For my family: To my grandparents, Doris and Ernie Smith and Eileen Williams, without whom I would not be living my dream, Linda Williams for being my mom, and brother Shane Williams for checking in and always being on my side. For Rod and Nancy Williams for making me a part of their family and for sending such lovely notes. For my uncle John Smith for inspiring me with his adventurous spirit and Joanne Adams for her love and support.

My heartfelt thanks goes out to my friends who are so much my family; Jennifer Little for hanging a picture of the Oscar on the wall back in grade 9 and never wavering from her dream—you are an inspiration. The Freud Sisters; Kelly Allison, Sara Rumsey, Lisa Butler. Helga Grau for being such a great Freud Sister in-training and for keeping her eyes on my path for me and opening up her home. Lisa Johnson, for sharing her heart. Maria Eftimiades for showing me how success and generosity fit together beautifully.

For Sandra Parker and the kitten. Kirsten Tisdale, Heather Mackenzie, Denise Rossetto for being women I admire. To George Salimes for sitting down on the bench next to me.

For all the Wildly Sophisticated women who write, call, and join us in sharing their career stories and to the inspiring women interviewed in this book for sharing their time and stories for all of us to share.

Introduction

When my agent called to suggest my next book should be focused on money, I almost fell out of my chair. Doesn't she know I haven't seen a "paycheck" in months after putting everything I have into my business? Isn't it obvious that I don't have a clue which stocks will yield the greatest return? Haven't I mentioned that I'm downright horrified by Suze Orman's suggestion to freeze my credit card? Forget about choosing a retirement fund—retirement? I just need a weekend off!

And then it hit me. These are exactly the reasons why this book should be focused on money. My life is no different than those of millions of women around the country who, just like you, are interested not in how to *save* more, but in how to *make* more—more out of our lives, more out of our careers, and more out of our earning potential.

And this is something I know a thing or two about.

Before we go any further, let me be clear. I'm not a financial planner. I don't have a degree in commerce. I cannot instruct you on how to make millions in the stock market or real estate. I have no interest in showing you how to balance your bankbook or save money.

What I am interested in is showing you how to invest in your life and in your career; how to earn more money and respect, how to evaluate your worth, how to ask for and get more, how to build influence, create greater independence, and even how to show you when credit card debt can actually work in your favor.

This is a career book focused on redefining investment, risk, and money, *not* a financial planning guidebook. I will discuss money—from saving to spending to investing—through the lens of career development and free-spirited entrepreneurialism. Wildly Sophisticated, the name of my company, exemplifies a brand, but more importantly describes an attitude that we all can share in creating career and financial success. It requires a willingness to try, an ability to focus, the drive to execute, and the passion to dream.

Just like *Wildly Sophisticated: A Bold New Attitude for Career Success,* I'm writing this book because I needed it. It's the book I was looking for. On some days I would look back at my career and into the future of my business and I couldn't figure out if I had it all together or I was totally and completely screwed. Is 100K too much to invest or not enough? Can I afford to take some time off? Is this experience about the money or the relationships I'm going to build? How do I create greater influence in the industry? What and who do I need to know? Is my rescue fantasy preventing me from jumping in with both feet? I've come to my answers through the process of writing this book and if you have similar kinds of queries, goals and, aspirations—so will you.

LANGUAGE OF DEBT AND SCARCITY

One of the things I disliked most about business-building and financial books already on the shelf was the language of scarcity, fear, and shortage. How to save? How to prevent bankruptcy? How to stay out of debt? How to start a business in tough times? This language didn't help me. In fact it scared the hell out of me . . . and it made me feel guilty. Nothing like reading about the importance of investing in your 401(k) when you've just invested your "extra" in that trademark application!

Here's the truth you're going to read about in this book—in a language that will not make you want to run directly into the arms of a rich, eighty-year-old geezer. There is no "right" time to launch a business. Debt is something you can use in your favor. You will have to invest both time and money in building a business—it's not something to be ashamed of, it's something to be proud of. "Debt" and "investment" are not about a dollar figure. While I don't underestimate the value of the stock market, the greatest stock you've got is *you* and I'm a firm believer that *you* are exactly where you need to start if you want to create wealth.

The reality is, in today's day and age, employer or no employer, you are a business owner—you own you and your career. Opportunity is limited only by what you're willing to invest in and of yourself. This is a liberating and abundant concept and it's yours for the taking.

My goal is to create a book that inspires you—that leaves you with a feeling of optimism and hope—rather than depletion and guilt. Another one of my goals is to share the uncommon advice and insight from women who are doing it, building success, right here and right now.

BEFORE NOT AFTER

You know about Madonna, Martha Stewart, and Carly Fiorina—you've heard their stories. They are compelling, inspiring, and downright motivating. But there are other women, women of our generation who are also blazing trails and pushing their limits in a way that will make you think— really, could that be possible at thirty-three?

With the intention of providing you with some fresh perspective for women who have not answered the "what inspires you" so many times that they've created a contrived answer. These women offer a level of authenticity and frankness that will help you to see your career in a new way. They are willing and able to open up and offer advice that feels relevant, fresh, and as per our goal, uncommon. This is what I wanted for this book.

"Before, not after" has become our guide. You will meet some extraordinary women thoughout the pages of this book. They offer insight on investment, lifestyle, and risk like you've never seen or heard before. I've invited Cheri Hanson, writer, freelance journalist, and director of content at Wildly Sophisticated Media to be a part of this project. Cheri sat down with these women who are in a full sprint toward "household" name status and asked them the questions I know you, too, would be dying to ask.

THE MILLION-DOLLAR QUESTION

Can you make a million bucks and feel worthless? Absolutely. But please know that a million bucks will never be enough. If you are earning and spending from a place of needing to fill the black hole of worthlessness, I promise you this: There are not enough Blahniks in the world.

Worth can create money but money, never, ever creates worth.

This book *is* about wealth, but let's be crystal clear: Wealth *is not* simply cold hard cash. When asked what they've learned about money, each and every one of the women we interviewed for this book responded with a variation of the same answer:

Money does not buy happiness.

Please put down this book knowing, the key to making more of your life—more money, more influence, more power—is believing you're worth more. Not a "yeah, I'm not bad" kind of belief. A full-on, you can't stop me kind of roar that starts in your stomach and cannot be suppressed. The kind of belief that compels you to go out there and get what you deserve. Before anyone is going to invest in you, you need to believe in your own worth. It's the first and most critical step in the wealth-building process.

How do you build wealth, power, and influence?

You learn how to earn what you're worth.

1

What Does Money Mean to Me?

How to Get a Grip

*I'm in the thick of a business deal with people I really like. People
I know. People I trust. People who, I believe, want the best for me
and for my business.*

*But more than the best for me, there's something else they
want.*

The best for themselves.

f there's only one thing that you take away from this book, please let it be
this. You need to look out for yourself when it comes to your money. Your
money is your responsibility.

You need to get a grip.

Even if you're the company superstar, I can guarantee you this: Your
boss is not sitting in her office thinking up ways to give you more money. It
doesn't matter how grateful she is for your incredible work and how many
people you've blown away with your brilliance—she will not be knocking on
your door one day, sheepishly asking you to consider a raise. Your investors
are not in partnership with you just because they think you're a nice person.

And if you're negotiating a mortgage or buying a car, the smiling guy across the desk will not bend over backward to get you the best rate. His job is to take as much money from you as possible. You've got to understand the way money works and you have to take care of yourself. No one else will do it for you.

In this chapter we will accomplish two things:

First, you'll decode your feelings about money—and figure out how those emotions are affecting your financial behavior. You have a unique relationship with your cash right here, right now. Dig deep. Face your fears and confront your fantasies. You might be surprised by what you learn.

Then, you'll learn how to build healthy relationships with the people who have influence over your cash. From the boss who's signing your checks to that bank manager who knows both you and your dog on a first-name basis, managing your money relationships requires finesse, but it will pay incredible dividends. Creating mutually beneficial relationships around money makes your life a whole lot simpler—and a whole lot wealthier.

But let's get one thing out of the way right now.

Money is hard. It's confusing. It's tangled up with your emotions, your values, your background, your relationships, and some seriously crazy and confusing cultural baggage. You can touch and feel money, but really, it's just a symbol. It's up to you to explore how you feel about money and to decide what money means to you. One of the easiest ways to slide into this topic is to examine your gut reactions to wealth—and to those who have it.

THE GUT REACTION

Paris and Nicky Hilton. Bill Gates. The Rockefellers. Donald Trump. Mary-Kate and Ashley Olsen.

What do all these people have in common? You guessed it: more money than they even know how to spend. What else do you think about these people, or anyone else with a private jet and a home on every continent? Are they:

Smart	**Cutthroat**	**Selfish**
Strong	**Spoiled**	**Generous**
Attractive	**Innovative**	**Inspiring**
Weak	**Deserving**	**Ugly**
Greedy	**Cruel**	**Disciplined**
Efficient	**Self-centered**	**Desirable**
Powerful	**Peaceful**	

Think honestly about how someone's net worth affects your assessment of his or her character. Next time you see that woman prancing down the street with a poodle decked out in Burberry or sliding out of a luxury car wrapped in fur, gauge your gut reactions. What are you thinking? How do you feel about her? Do you step aside so she can avoid the slushy part of the sidewalk?

By examining your feelings about people who have lots of money, you can begin to understand your own beliefs about wealth and prosperity. This sounds a lot easier than it actually is, especially if you're truly being honest with yourself.

I've done this exercise both with people who proclaim to hate money and with those who love it. Those who hate money use the words *greedy, selfish,* and *egotistical* to describe people with cash in their pockets. Those who love money use words like *intelligent, focused, savvy,* and *enterprising.*

This isn't rocket science. Do your own little case study: Start listening to the way people talk about money; make note of contradictions. I have a friend who is downright desperate for money. Says he wants it. Says he needs it. But whenever he talks about people with cash, it's with disdain, suspicion, and, more often than not, he says outright that "They don't deserve it." Here's the secret: He's not talking about others; he's talking about himself. He doesn't feel as if he deserves money and until he does, he won't have any.

Now apply this concept to yourself. Observing how you react to wealthy people is a direct link to your core beliefs about money. You need to be honest with yourself in order to start to rework your feelings about money. One of the best ways of getting to the root of your money issues is to examine the foundations.

Where do we get our money perceptions? Look first and foremost to your family.

Did you grow up with money?

Did you feel as if you had as much as you needed?

Did you feel deprived?

How did your parents relate to money?

How did your parents talk about people with money or without it?

How was money used in relation to reward and punishment?

Next, examine all the big money "experiences" of your life. I have a client who remembers, as a kid, approaching the apartment where she and her mom lived, only to find an eviction notice on the door and the locks changed. They had a police escort for the thirty minutes they were given to pack up their belongings. You're not going to be surprised that, as an adult, she lives with a six-month protective nest egg to ensure that, in her words, "that never, ever, ever happens again."

> I can live without money, but I cannot live without love.
> —Judy Garland

Your money experiences can be anything from getting burned by working your ass off only to not get paid, to the exhilaration of a raise, or to the first time you bought anything with your own money. Make a list of all the memorable experiences you've had with money and what you learned about money through these experiences. This exercise is immensely helpful in unearthing the ways in which you relate to, and experience money.

Our ingrained attitudes about money—and about those who already have a lot of it—are worth exploring for one important reason. Without a healthy attitude toward money, you have little chance of ever really accumulating much of it.

If you have a fundamental belief that people with money are greedy, the likelihood that you're ever going to earn "riches"—in any capacity—is limited.

WHAT'S YOUR WHY?

It's a movie cliché. The glamorous couple robs a bank (or hits it big at the casino, or steals the mobster's suitcase of money . . .) and spreads the bills all over the bed, rolling over the cash in a passionate embrace. The message: Money is sexy, desirable, and money makes you happy (at least for a fleeting moment).

I don't know about you, but the concept of actually rolling around in money is more than a little revolting. It's not the actual bills we're after; it's what we actually want our money to provide for us. For most of us, it's not a pair of shoes or a vacation home at the shore—not really. What we really want from money is more intangible. One of the most effective ways of both understanding how we relate to money and ensuring we continue to make more of it, is to clearly define *why* we want money in the first place.

I went through a period where I was investing everything I had in my business. Regardless of the fact that I was earning more for the company than I ever had before, personally I was feeling financially depleted. I kept making financial goals for my business (I'll sell this show for x amount), thinking that once I reached the target, my personal financial distress would dissipate. It didn't. I kept reliving this cycle until I was literally facing a million-dollar deal and personal bankruptcy at the exact same moment.

I sat back and asked myself, How in the world did I feel more financially stable after I graduated from university and made twenty-eight thousand a year? I came to realize that it's not just about the dollar figure—it's about your "why." Why do you want money? What purpose do you want money to serve in your life? I discovered that, for me, money is about taking risks and living an adventurous life around my passion for women and work, but on a personal level it's also about freedom and comfort—neither of which I had experienced for the last three years. No, I didn't want to choose bankruptcy. But I also had to decide if I wanted the million dollars that would mean an incredible time commitment, an unrelenting travel schedule, and limitations on other parts of my business that I enjoy more.

You don't have to be an entrepreneur to be faced with money decisions.

An investment in a course, your willingness to negotiate a raise, a pay cut, in order to work with someone you respect and can learn from—these are financial decisions that cross industries and job descriptions. Your career will be filled with financially oriented decisions at every stage.

I've saved the most important point for last: Your *why* is always evolving. It responds to the complex mix of emotions, experiences, and desires in your life. After a tough year or a serious personal challenge, you may crave security over adventure. If you've been feeling stagnant at work with a constant eye on the clock, risk and freedom may get top billing. You've got to keep checking in with yourself and asking the question, "What's my why?" Earning more money is about choices, and in order to make choices, you need to understand what you want.

What's your why?

The Big Four

There are four major "whys" I hear from women across the board. Maybe they'll feel familiar to you.

Comfort

I want to live comfortably.

I want money to buy an apartment of my own.

I want to be able to enjoy a nice dinner out or get a pedicure now and then.

Security

I don't want to wake up in the middle of the night panicked and worrying about how I'm going to pay my rent.

I want to have some stability, some sense of ease that will allow me to pursue my dreams without an impending sense of doom and destitution.

I want to take good care of my family.

Freedom

> I don't want to have to answer to anyone.
>
> I'm tired of owing the bank, my parents, the government—my whole life feels like it's on loan.
>
> I don't want anyone telling me when to come and go. I want to work on my own clock.

Adventure/Risk

> I want to be able to use my money to build more.
>
> I want to invest in my career. I want to invest in my future.
>
> I want to travel—and be my own boss.

WOMEN AND MONEY

As a career manager, I work primarily with women, so I may be biased about this. But it seems to me that women have issues with money that men don't struggle with, at least not to the same degree. And based upon the "case studies" below, it's not as if the challenges stop once you've got your hot little hands on the big money. Even high-profile women who aren't lacking cash still deal with some serious money issues.

> Isn't privacy about keeping taboos in their place?
> —Kate Millet

Please take two key ideas away from this section. One, you're not alone. We're all struggling to get a grip, no matter what our bank balances look like. Two, we've got to overcome all the negative emotions. Guilt, shame, secrecy, embarrassment—these are obstacles on the road to creating more. Overcome them now, and you'll be ready to enjoy the wealth you create and to share it, with abundance and freedom.

I Don't Want to Talk About It

According to *The Guinness Book of World Records,* Cameron Diaz holds the record for the highest yearly earnings of any actress—ever. In 2001, she made $41 million, and she earned an estimated $45 million in 2003. Industry reports say she's paid anywhere between $10 and $20 million per film.

Sounds good? It is, but it's also none of our business, said Cameron in an interview with *W* magazine: "There are a lot of things I *wouldn't* do [even] for $20 million—an amount of money that is now disclosed to the entire world." She called the public knowledge of her salary "the rudest thing ever . . . I mean, I don't go around asking anyone else what they make for a living."

> I make a lot of money but I don't want to talk about that. I work very hard and I'm worth every cent.
>
> —Naomi Campbell

When it comes to money, everyone wants to know, but very few women want to tell. So why is the topic of money taboo? I've had this discussion with friends, women in my office, my mom, and it's been really difficult to put a finger on it. In search of further explanation, I looked up the origin of the word *taboo* in *Encyclopedia Britannica,* and this is what I found: "Most authorities agree that they [taboos] tend to relate to objects and actions that are significant for the maintenance of social order."

I'm not a big "conspiracy theory" kind of girl, but isn't that interesting? I'd argue that women, more than men, are far less prone to talk about their financial lives. And as long as we're not talking, we're not asking questions and not gaining important information—information like: "How did you negotiate that raise?" "How do you find a credit card with a lower interest rate?" "How can I get through Christmas this year without going totally broke?" If we start talking, we can take away some of the "forbidden" aspects of money and change the social order.

Am I suggesting you ask your new boyfriend, "So, what do you make?" Maybe. If it helps you to question why, as a teacher, you're making 30 grand a year versus his 150 grand as a financial analyst, then, by all means. But talking about money doesn't mean you have to ask deeply personal questions or make your friends and family *really* uncomfortable. Some money issues *are* personal, but cloaking all money discussion in secrecy implies there's something we need to hide, something that we shouldn't be talking about. In reality, by opening up and talking about issues that scare us, opportunities that have surprised us, and experiences that we can all learn from, we *all* benefit.

Money Makes Me Feel Guilty

We can all take a lesson from Oprah Winfrey in the guilt department. Having amassed a fortune that would keep a small country running for years, Oprah states proudly: "I have never felt a moment of guilt about what I have."

Unfortunately, Oprah is not the norm. When it comes to working with women, I've noticed that there's real trepidation in stating outright that they want to make money. When asked why, the resounding response is because they feel guilty and greedy. One client put it this way, "Living the dream or making money, it's like you have to choose one or the other. Wanting money implies that you've sold out."

Why is it that so many men have no problem raking in the cash, but wealthy women feel they have to apologize for their riches—even when they've worked like dogs to earn it? There's no denying it: Money is power. We're just beginning to enter the era of trophy husbands and female-dominated boardrooms. Women are everywhere men are, there just aren't as many of us at the top. When women have money, choices, and power, it disturbs the status quo.

Do you feel guilty about wanting money? Do you feel guilty about the money you have earned? How does guilt stop you from making more?

I Don't Deserve Money

I was watching a documentary about Canadian singer/songwriter Jann Arden as she toured the United States. In one scene, Jann talked about her struggles with her feelings about money and her worth. She related a conversation with her father who said, "Jann, you made more money this year than I've made in my whole life." As she wiped away the tears, Jann said she didn't know whether to laugh, cry, or get in her car and just keep driving.

You could see it in Jann's face. You know she's worked hard for her money, you know she's talented, funny, smart, strong—the whole package. But you could see that her father's question made her wonder, "Why me? Do I deserve the money?"

The answer is yes, yes, and yes again. And answering yes doesn't mean that her father didn't work just as hard—or harder—than his wealthy daughter, or that he didn't deserve financial rewards of his own. We all deserve to achieve our dreams. Whether or not money actually materializes is another discussion. We're all deserving. Full stop. Take deserving out of the equation and move forward.

I'm Afraid of Money

How much money is in your wallet right now? Your bank account? How much money do you have on your credit card? How far are you into your line of credit? If you can't answer these questions, you may have a fear issue around money. Why would anyone be afraid of money, you ask? It sounds crazy, I know, but it's surprisingly common. Here are what financial fears can look like.

There Will Never Be Enough
Have you ever heard about someone winning ten grand and you think, "that wouldn't even put a dent in my debt." Fear of there never being enough is one of the primary issues that keeps us from truly facing our reality. We feel hopeless, almost as if tackling our financial life wouldn't even help. In most cases, those who live with this fear don't have a clue as to what enough is, and they don't have a solid sense of their own financial reality.

I've Got a Death Grip

I'm sure you've been here. A friend's birthday dinner. Great food and wine. Lots of laughs. Bill time rolls around and the head of the table divides up the bill evenly. And you can't believe your ears: "But I didn't order a dessert."

Some people will grasp every penny as if it were their last. One of the basic principles of creating wealth is to be generous with what you've got and to believe that you can always gain back what you've lost. A fear of losing money will impede your ability to take risks— one of the most powerful ways of creating wealth.

> I can't think of anything I want and need that I don't already have but at the same time, I'm not sated.
>
> —Ashley Judd

I Don't Wanna Look

If we're talking about fear, we're also talking about control, or the lack of it.

Let me guess. You know exactly how many calories are in one large bagel or a medium-sized glass of wine. You can map out a fitness routine from magazines, friends, and some keen observation at the gym. Between yoga, Pilates, and vitamin supplements, you manage your body like a high-performance vehicle. But your bank accounts? The statement arrives and you stuff it in the drawer. It's the ultimate avoidance. But by *not* taking charge of your money, you're actually letting it control you.

I've met a lot of women out there who are afraid to make money, afraid not to make money, afraid to negotiate for more money, afraid to spend the money they have, afraid to save the money they've got.

It's worth repeating. One of the most important things you can do with your financial situation is to face it—to get a grip on your fears. It is scary. But just like facing anything that makes your heart race a mile a minute, the reality is often not as bad as you're anticipating, and even if it is, an honest understanding will help empower you to make changes. At the very least, you'll have the freedom that comes with knowing the truth.

RESCUE FANTASIES

No judgment here. Based on conversations I've had with my friends, coworkers and young women around the country, everyone has a rescue fantasy of some sort. And let's face it, when you're pushing your limits—with your money, your work, your goals—some of these scenarios start looking pretty attractive. It just takes one brutal day to reignite your daydreams about that nerdy guy from chem class who was destined to be a billionaire. After all, he did have a crush on you during high school . . .

Don't worry. Rescue fantasies are generally harmless, and they can be a great way to figure out your money "weak spots"—the subtle ways you might be avoiding full control of your life or your money. The fantasy only gets dangerous if you're really, really counting on that scratch-and-win ticket to pay your bills.

Here are some of the most common rescue fantasies out there:

Prince Charming in a Porsche
(AKA The man with the money)

Some of the strongest, most independent women I know still have this nagging sense that their financial situation isn't quite real. Someone else is out there, waiting to take them away from all that nasty credit card debt. You know what I'm talking about. You met this investment banker last night, and he just may be the handsome answer to your financial troubles. Now, it's not like you're Anna Nicole Smith. You don't have to be cosying up to an eighty-nine-year-old oil baron to understand the Prince Charming fantasy. It's all about love, but ideally it comes in a wealthy package.

The Million-Dollar Screenplay
(AKA The stroke of genius that will make you rich, rich, rich)

This is a common one. It's also the fuel that fires reality TV and pyramid schemes everywhere. Your genius fantasy could involve anything from writing the Great American Novel to getting famous for your fabulous singing voice. The bottom line is this: You have an incredible talent that, once revealed, will pay millions and put in you in limos and at the top of Oscar-party invitation lists.

The Family Windfall
(AKA Great-Aunt Doris stashed major cash in her mattress)

This scenario can go two ways:

One: A totally unknown, ridiculously wealthy family member leaves you a fat inheritance check. You didn't even know you had a Great-Aunt Doris, but luckily, she knew all about you.

Two: Every time you've maxed out your MasterCard, your family was there to help. Regardless of whether that help came with strings attached, or it was freely and graciously given, you've come to rely on your relatives. Deep down, you believe Daddy will always swoop in and make it better. This is a common (if not often-discussed) fantasy that's especially potent when you come from wealth and abundance.

My Brilliant Stockbroker
(AKA Those Enron shares are going to soar)

You can sniff a great investment from a mile away. Problem is, you smell the questionable ones from six feet. That's why your stockbroker (or brother, or father-in-law, or deli guy) is giving you tips that can't lose. We've all heard tales of ground-floor stock purchases that turned, literally, into gold. You know it's gambling, but hey, you're a winner. Why should this be any different? All you need is a good chunk of change to invest . . .

The Winning Ticket
(AKA Life after the lottery)

Scratch-and-win, slot machines, super-prize draws, Vegas—there's a reason so many of us fantasize about beating the odds and escaping to Ibiza. It's gotta be the most straightforward rescue fantasy out there. Invest two dollars, wait a few days, and head back to the 7-Eleven with your winning ticket. Ditch your beat-up wheels and leave in a limo.

Head in the Sand
(AKA It's good to be an ostrich)

Why bother saving for the future? And what's all this talk of 401(k)s? Everyone knows the only constant is change. When my retirement party rolls around, nothing will be the same, so I'm just going to wait and see what happens. At the very worst, the government will be there to help, right?

The best way to get past all this emotional quicksand is to have a solid understanding of your own feelings. By figuring out what you really think and feel about money, you can move forward and deal with your cash in ways that are smart and sane. This is a really crucial step, because it ensures that you're standing on solid ground.

Your money fantasies, fears, and misconceptions are most effectively countered by facing the cold hard facts, and unless you're able and willing to actually dedicate some intimate one-on-one time with your cash, you're never going to get there.

> Whoever said money can't buy happiness simply didn't know where to go shopping.
>
> —Bo Derek

MAKE A DATE WITH YOUR MONEY

You have a living, breathing relationship with your money. And just as any great relationship relies on trust, respect, honesty, commitment, and sharing, so does the way you interact with your cash. If you were to take a poll of every financially successful person you know, the one common denominator you'd discover is that they spend quality time with their cash.

Sound complicated? It's not. What I'm suggesting here is that you and your bank statements sit down over a soda-and-cranberry for some quality time together. Start today and mark this as your anniversary. Pay your bills. Make a budget, then analyze how your spending stacks up against that budget. Go through all your credit card statements and major transactions. Set financial goals for yourself and create a roadmap to get you there.

But remember, while your anniversary date may be when you explore your long-term plans, it's the way you relate to your money day to day that makes all the difference. Your money relationship requires commitment, communication, and ongoing effort. Ever notice how little squabbles with your boyfriend can eventually blow up into a full-on fight? The same goes for your money. Take care of the details, and you'll be looking at a long, happy future together. Here are the essential elements you need for a great relationship with your cash:

Respect

Have a coupon in your purse but you're too embarrassed to pull it out? Walk past a quarter but you're too lazy to pick it up? Don't ask for a discount for fear of being perceived as cheap? Tip 15 percent even in the face of awful service? These are just a few of the ways we disrespect money. If you want to create a better relationship with your money, respect it.

Honesty

I was attending a workshop a couple of years ago where we were asked to look at some of the challenges in our life and to examine our true intentions. I decided to consider my financial life. After an honest exploration of the question, it hit me that my intention was to look rich. I was choosing to buy the Fendi bag (to look like I had money) rather than putting the cash toward my credit card debt (to actually have money). I was a bit taken aback and embarrassed by this revelation, but if I hadn't been honest with myself, I would be living in the same cycle of financial delusion.

Your relationship with money thrives on honesty. You need to think through, very honestly, what money means to you and ask yourself what your intentions are toward your money. You need to face your financial situation—truthfully. And most importantly, you need to be upfront about what you have and what you don't have, with the rest of the world. More than anything else, the intention to look rich will prevent you from actually being rich.

Effort

Just like anything worth having, your relationship with money requires work and commitment. One of the "relationship-with-money" issues I see most often is laziness. *"I can't be bothered to do my expenses tonight. I can't hit that 401(k) presentation after work, I've got a date. My bank is another block away, so I'll use this ATM."*

Financial success requires commitment and hard work. Buck up.

Trust

Sometimes, our relationship with money looks like a one-way street. "I'm doing all the work" is an exasperated whine I hear regularly. It's not true. If you're working for your money, you have to trust that your money is working for you, even if it doesn't always look that way. Just like any long-standing relationship, there are will be hard times. Times when you wonder if it's worth it. Times when you wonder if your "partner" is deserving of your time and commitment. Maybe you're following all the rules and you're still going through financial hard times. You're saving to buy an apartment. You're investing in your business and taking a meager paycheck. Trust that, with a solid foundation, this is a relationship that will work out for the best.

Abundance

I'm going to tell you a story that I don't think even I would believe if I hadn't experienced it myself. I was at the hardest financial point in my professional life. I was dollars away from bankruptcy. Walking out of the bank, I found myself face to face with a man strumming a guitar with his open case empty of change. Our eyes met, and I felt compelled to share what I had.

I walked into a meeting, turned off my cell phone and didn't think any more about it. When I came out of my meeting, I turned on my phone to find a message that I had been awarded a six-figure contract. Did this change of fate occur because I had experienced a feeling of abundance in the face of scarcity? Who knows, but I've come to hear enough of these stories to know that the more you give, the more you get. It's the karma of all relationships and it's equally true of your bank account. Money is dynamic and it flows. You need to give it away to get it back in return.

These relationship tips are not just about you and your cash. They also apply to the people in your life who can help you invest, save, and make more of your money. After you and your bankbook get cozy, it's time to introduce some others into the mix. Your boss, your banker, your accountant, even your family and friends if they've spotted you some cash—these are money relationships that need to be approached with the same level of respect, trust, and honesty as you've just applied to your own financial situation.

YOUR MONEY RELATIONSHIPS

Just as you're not going to get married on your first date, the likelihood of your boss offering you a raise your first day on the job or your banker signing a check an hour after your first visit is somewhere between slim and none. Money relationships are incredibly important both for creating a healthy financial life and getting a grip on your money. Your money is your responsibility, and a part of that responsibility is to ensure that you have the support you need.

Before you can earn and accomplish what you want with your money, spend a little time thinking about who you know, and how they've influenced you. Did your parents promise to help you pay tuition and then they backed out at crunch time? Does your accountant double as your therapist? No matter how tight you are with your money, *your relationship doesn't live in a vacuum.* And unlike most committed relationships, you and your cash will actually benefit from a little outside action. Mix it up. Keep it interesting. Just remember who you're going home with at the end of the night.

Boss and Employers

Let's be crystal clear about this. Your boss—that woman who signs your checks and conducts your performance review—she's a money relationship. Unless you're working for free (and quite frankly, even if you are) this relationship is critical in creating more.

Here's a tip that underpins your money relationship with your boss. All business relies on the trade of goods and/or services for money. Just like you, your boss is getting paid for the performance of duties. And get this—in many instances, her bottom line is tied to your performance. The key to making more is to understand how your efforts are directly attached to your boss's income.

Here's a more simplistic example. Maybe you're selling cosmetics at Sephora. Your boss (the store manager/owner) is your link to more work and an ongoing paycheck. But, if you can figure out a way to energize yourself and your coworkers, sell more products, and build stronger customer relationships, you're going to generate more revenue for the store, and for your boss. The bottom line? You've laid the groundwork to earn more money for yourself, and short of a raise or some profit-sharing, you'll still have earned her trust, respect and loyalty—amazing rewards that you'll be able to leverage now and in the future.

Friends and Family

For the most part, our first brush with financial relationships came when our parents pulled out a weekly five-dollar bill in exchange for making our bed and throwing a load of laundry into the dryer. Our family is one of the first places we learn how to manage both our money and our financial relationships. Once we move past the allowance stage of our lives, our families may play a role in contributing toward tuition, underwriting our first credit card, or buying our first place. This is when you need to be more careful.

There are two primary stumbling blocks in familial money relationships. One, we treat them differently than our other, more formal, financial relationships. We don't always pay our debt on time, we put our family loan payment on the bottom of the priority pile, or in the back of our minds we think, "They'll eventually let me

> I don't have a boyfriend right now. I'm looking for anyone with a job who I don't have to support.
> —Anna Nicole Smith

off." In short, we lack respect for this money-based relationship, thinking "Hey, they're family!"

The other problem is a lack of communication. The terms are not clearly defined from the outset. Expectations are not met and neither party is talking for fear of causing a major upset. Over time, trust gets broken and resentment builds. Money issues within families have the potential to cause catastrophic breakups. You need to be *more* aware and respectful of your family money relationships—*not less*. There is a tremendous amount at stake.

Banker

This is an obvious one, but it's surprisingly underexplored, underutilized, and undernourished. I know it can sometimes be difficult to forge relationships in your bank, considering the basic "teller turnover" rate. Follow the Go Big concept and you'll win this one. One important point that people tend to forget with financial institutions (considering what they're charging us in hidden service fees and all) is that they're working for you. Ask to speak with the manager—the more senior she is, the closer she'll be to real decision-making power and to real cash. These people are less likely to be leaving next month.

Why should you build a personal relationship with your banker, even if you're not starting a business or looking for a loan? Because you never know what's down the road. Maybe you'll want to buy a home and take out a mortgage. Or maybe you'll want to start an investment account for your new baby. The top brass at your bank branch have the power to push the rules a little. We're talking lower interest rates, better loan terms, and fewer service fees. I can't promise anything, but it pays to become more than just an anonymous account number—before you actually need something from your bank.

If you don't know how to start the relationship, make an appointment to go through your current accounts, credit cards, and any other services you have with the company. It doesn't matter if you're still working on that single checking account, you can open the conversation by asking questions about your money. Is this the best checking plan for me? Could I benefit from a flat-rate monthly service charge? If you're interested, your banker will be too. Remember, they want to keep your business, and the better you do, the more cash you'll be unloading into their vaults.

Financial Planners

This is where it starts to get sticky, and where you've got to do your homework. A financial planner reviews all elements of your financial situation—investments, taxes, insurance, retirement and savings strategies, estate planning, etc.—and creates a personalized plan to help you achieve your money goals. Planners can be valuable because they look at your financial life in totality. They're not just focused on your bank accounts or your income tax. If you need help with your money on a broad scale, this is a great relationship to nurture.

There are three ways financial planners are paid: hourly fees, through a combination of fees and commissions (from selling you specific insurance and/or investment products), and by commission only.

While there are thousands of fully qualified, objective planners who have your best interests at heart, there are also a lot of quacks, financially speaking. The best place to find a Certified Financial Planner (CFP)—a globally recognized professional designation that requires specific education, experience, and ethical standards—is through the International Certified Financial Planning Council. You can visit their website at www.fpsb.org. The International CFP Council has more than 80,000 members worldwide. Personal referrals are also a great way to find a planner. If a friend, family member, or colleague has a trusted planner, you may want to start there.

Accountants

Mastered your income tax forms? Employed full time? Figure you don't need an accountant? Think again. You don't have to be an entrepreneur to benefit from tax advice. From the course bill you footed, to treating your mentor to a coffee, legitimate work-related expenses have the potential to offset your income and save you tax dollars.

But there's more to consider when you're dealing with an accountant. Unlike a banker or some financial planners, an accountant has no stake in your money. She'll charge an hourly rate for meetings, services, and advice. She wants you to succeed, simply so she can continue to help manage your money. And managing is the key here. Despite their high profile at tax time, accountants are also highly knowledgeable about other aspects of your financial life. They can help you plan an overall strategy for saving, spending, investing, and beyond. Unlike a broker or another, more specialized financial professional, accountants offer another take on the whole picture and can help you make decisions that truly fit your life.

One of the first and most important money relationships I developed was with my accountant. Tax rules and regulations change with the blink of an eye. Between write-offs, deductions, and shelters, your accountant can save you thousands of dollars. This is one relationship that absolutely requires honesty. Who knows your financial life better? It also requires trust. Selecting an accountant is one part certification and two parts gut feel.

Investors

Think big picture. It doesn't matter what you do for a living, your investors include anyone and everyone who want to see you succeed. These are the people who are *invested* in your success. Your long-time mentor, that encouraging college professor, your former boss who wrote a glowing reference letter—it pays to pull together a list of your biggest fans and supporters.

We're going to talk a lot about investment later in the book, but even if you've got a full lineup of wealthy shareholders for your new yoga studio, let's be clear—it's not all about the cash. My business partners invested months of time and energy in me *before* they ever gave me a dime. Investment is a two-way street, and it's not only applicable to business owners. You want to make sure you're getting something real out of these relationships. Your investors have an enormous capacity to do more than whip out the checkbook—look for expertise, introductions, and some great advice.

Getting Serious

Here are three critical issues to cover before taking all these money relationships to second base.

Start Early

You want to be building your money relationships long before you *need* them. Time is the key to building trust and illustrating commitment—the basis of these relationships. Setting up your first meeting with a banker on the day you're applying for a mortgage, for example, is not in your best interest. Financial situations come up in life at surprising times and if you've got a long-standing, nurtured relationship, it is more likely you'll be able to access what you need.

Check the Frames on the Wall

Without question your first step is to examine the paperwork. Is this person certified? I meet a lot of women who approach their financial relationships as they would the guy at customs or the cop who has pulled them over—with fear and trepidation. This is your *hire*. You are purchasing this person's services. You have every right, and in fact it is your responsibility, to look long and hard at the individual's qualifications. Ask to speak with past clients and check with the Better Business Bureau.

Clearly Define Expectations

Money often comes attached to family and friends, and while a bank will require a term sheet that clearly defines expectations, friends, family, and even some vendors usually don't—and this is a mistake. You might even meet a lawyer who loves your business concept, who really believes in you, and who offers some consultation for free. Jackpot—for about four months, until your revenue finally starts rolling in. Suddenly, you've got a bill for five thousand dollars, based on what he thought was the agreement. Mutual understanding (without writing) looks a lot different to one person than it will to another.

MONEY NOT WORTH TAKING

I can't leave this chapter without talking about bad money relationships. Hear me when I say this. There is some money that's not worth having. And it's not about the actual cash, it's about the person giving it to you. I'll give you an example. Business people are always trying to hook you up with other business people. For the most part, this works in your favor. If you get in with someone who is well connected (which should be the goal), they will shop you around town, facilitating introductions and great meetings. But it doesn't take long to identify whose referrals you want, and whose you really don't.

I was in New York, and a business associate had set up a meeting with a prominent corporate player who potentially could have helped my business enormously. He was attending a conference close to Central Park, and with only a few minutes for me, we took at quick walk down the street and sat on a bench to chat. Initially, everything seemed normal. Ten minutes turned into twenty, and twenty turned into thirty. His questions became increasingly personal, and—I know you know this feeling—I could just tell there was something all wrong about this guy. As we stood up to go our separate ways, he left me with a wink and said, "You seem like the kind of girl who would do anything to succeed."

This guy could have written me a check for a million bucks and it wouldn't have been worth it. There are some money relationships that you don't want to go near, that will cost you in the end. Trust your gut.

"That's nice and all but . . . it's all about dollars and cents. More has got to come in than goes out."

I pulled this sentence from an e-mail I received yesterday from a business partner. It's always as I'm about to forget the fact that my business partners are not my friends that I'll get a poignant reminder.

The most interesting thing about money is that we first need to personalize it—we need to understand why we want it, explore our rescue fantasies, get a grip on how it makes us feel— and then we need to depersonalize it in order to make sound financial decisions, especially in conjunction with your money relationships.

Business and financial partnerships, connections and relationships are not always easy. There are losers. There comes a point when you, your money, and your business have to mean more to you than being liked or accepted. Money is tough, there's no question about it, but in order to create wealth you've got no choice.

You've got to get a grip.

wildly sophisticated icons

✳ Cheyann Benedict and Claire Stansfield

Cofounders, C&C California

It all started with the quest for the perfect T-shirt. Something soft, lived-in, sexy, and comfortable—and it wasn't on the market. Now Cheyann Benedict and Claire Stansfield run a multimillion-dollar design company and see their shirts on celebrities, including Jennifer Aniston, Courteney Cox, and Sofia Coppola. Their popsicle-bright, made-for-layering T-shirts were even featured on *Oprah*'s "Favorite Things" show. After investing twenty thousand dollars of their own cash, Claire and Cheyann have now built C&C into a multimillion-dollar company.

Part of C&C's enviable success lies in how the shirts cross variations in taste, age, and body type. Claire—a former actor who played the villainous Alti on *Xena: Warrior Princess*—is extremely tall and lanky. Cheyann—a photographer-turned-fashion retailer—is a petite Size 0. C&C shirts work for both of them, and these fashion-minded friends have built a growing empire based on passion, determination, and unbeatable instincts.

✳ Claire Stansfield

What's the best investment you've ever made?
The ten thousand dollars I put into making these T-shirts, and the time it's taken to see that investment through. It has literally changed my life. It's very lucrative—we've made quite a bit of money—and I feel strongly that we'll continue to grow and change. And now, I also have a completely different lifestyle. I really enjoy waking up and going to work. I love having this company to run.

From a business sense, everyone said that everything we were doing was wrong. I had a collection of sewing kits from hotels that my mother (a flight attendant) had gone to, and Cheyann worked in retail to help get herself through school, but all in all, we had zero fashion background. But we knew T-shirts. It's basic construction, so it was easy to draw and have patterns made, but it was the whole philosophy and the fabric and the feel that made the idea new, and that was what everybody said was wrong. In our entire process, we do everything that you're not supposed to do. But we test our T-shirts, we live in them, and we don't make anything that Cheyann and I don't covet and love to wear, or something that we feel is missing from our wardrobes. We're really just making things that we love. It's like anything—if you love it a lot and you do it, you're going to get good at it.

What has influenced your professional success?
I'm lucky that Cheyann and I were both at this stage in our lives where it was a "do or die" mentality. We know we both want a certain lifestyle and we both want to be our own bosses and create an environment, and we are not stopping until we can create that for ourselves. So if something doesn't work or if something is too difficult, there is nothing stopping us. We never say, "Oh, let's give up."

What has been the hardest thing for you to learn about money?
That it changes people. I think 99 percent of the people in my life are extremely happy for us, and really supportive, but I think for some people, our success just reminds them of what they still want to do. They'll say, "Wow, a year ago you were renting a tiny cabin in Laurel Canyon and you were driving around in your tiny used car and now, you just bought a house and a brand-new Range Rover and oooh, look at you. I could do that." And they don't realize it's a combination of all kinds of doors opening. All my PR connections and friends and relationships that I've cultivated for over twenty years, and a lot of hard work, so it didn't just happen overnight. But people always think that it did. There were moments—we call them our "hold me" moments—where literally things were so hard, and it felt like going into a battle. You'd come out of it and say, "Oh my God, did we really just do that?" And I think that's the key to success. You have to fight and fight hard.

What are the best money relationships you've built?

With our company, it's a fifty/fifty partnership. Everything is fifty/fifty, whether it's remembering that you put a quarter in the parking meter just now, so I'll get you next time. Even though we're a multimillion-dollar company, we still keep it that basic. Cheyann does all of the deposits and I do all of the check writing, so there is always a check system where she knows what's going in and I know what's going out. And one can't work without the other. I mean, I can't write checks without deposits going in, and when she's depositing, she's always aware of what's in there. And I have to tell her what goes out so that she can make sure there's enough in there. So there is a check system that makes us need to trust each other.

✳ Cheyann Benedict

What do you think is the greatest misconception people have about money?

That it will inflate your self-esteem. I read an interview with Alanis Morrisette a while ago where she said one of the reasons she wanted to become a pop star was because she thought she'd make all this money and her self-esteem would go way up—and I can tell you from experience, it just doesn't. I never thought, "Okay, my self-esteem is going to soar and millions of people are going to tell me that they love me," and not that I want those things, but on some level, it's in your head. The funny thing is, no matter how much money I make, I'm still the same person. I'm the *exact same person.*

Do you have a rescue fantasy?

There have been days and weeks when I've worked so hard, I've been so tired. And I still have days where I'm like, "Man, why can't I just meet a rich guy? I'd be laying out in the Bahamas right now." So, even with a little financial security, I still have this rescue fantasy.

How do you feel about debt?

I've often been in debt. One of the things I love doing now is paying off my credit card debt from when I was living off a meager income. But that debt never really bothered me because that was an investment in my future. I'm not afraid of debt because I am not afraid to work. I am not afraid of work because I have never had a problem getting a job. I have a very strong work ethic.

What have you had to learn about money?

With my personality, working for other people is difficult. Maybe it's because when I was growing up, both of my parents owned their own companies, so I didn't like the idea of working for someone else. So, I did things when I was young to make it so that I wouldn't have to work for other people. The first thing I did was buy a really, really inexpensive 400-square-foot apartment in New York. When I went to rent it out, I got a really good rate for it. I had a little bit of inheritance and I spent it all on this little apartment. I didn't save any to live off of, I just said, "Here is something tangible to help my future." I invested in property and became a landlord, and I didn't have a lot of income in the bank, but I had these things that made money so I wouldn't have to punch a clock.

2

-- -- -- -- --

What Am I Worth?

Identifying Your Tangibles

George Bernard Shaw said, "There are two great disappointments in life. Not getting what you want and getting it."

One of the most significant, life-changing experiences I have ever had was to actually achieve the goal that I had strived, sacrificed, and persevered for, only to find disappointment on the other side. I had somehow bought into the myth that with money, status, and power I would finally feel as if I had "arrived"—that I was worthy.

I was wrong.

So here's the good news and the bad news—your ability to create wealth directly corresponds with what you actually believe you're worth. From the West Coast to the East, one of the biggest traps so many of us seem to be living in is the "when-I-make-more-I-will-be-worth-more" reversal that couldn't be farther from reality.

> **Success is like reaching an important birthday and finding you're exactly the same.**
>
> —Audrey Hepburn

Please hear me. The first and most important

factor in building wealth comes from a solid feeling of worth that is NOT attached to a dollar figure.

Before you even begin to think about negotiating a raise, a promotion, or approaching a bank for a business loan, you need to have a long, hard look at your education, skills, talents, experience, integrity, confidence, and even your level of discipline. These attributes, not your bank balance, are the true foundation of your worth.

In these next two chapters, I'll discuss how an honest assessment of your worth is the secret to success—giving you the understanding and the commitment to pursue more money, more respect, more control, and more influence in your career and your life as a whole.

WHAT ARE YOU WORTH?

What I know for sure is that you can't sell what you don't believe in. And regardless of whether you are an entrepreneur, an executive, or an artist, in this marketplace, the most valuable commodity you have to sell is YOU.

What are you worth?

While the rest of this book is all about translating your worth into value so you can make more, we're going to start by focusing wholly and completely on you.

Your Personal Balance Sheet

I'm going to be honest. I wrote this entire chapter describing all the tangible assets and submitted a draft to my editor. Her note back: "So where is the Balance Sheet exercise? Is it a pullout at the back of the book?"

Damn, she noticed. The reality is, I wasn't quite sure how to lay it out. Does this strategy center on a pie chart? Do I insert a graph at the end of each section? Should there be a rating scale? In frustration, I pulled out a blank piece of paper, positioned it horizontally, and simply divided it into six categories and

> Your worth consists in what you are and not in what you have.
>
> —Thomas A. Edison

wrote each tangible attribute at the top of the page. Then I dove in.

Under Unique Experiences, I wrote down studying in Russia, traveling by myself to Nepal, being invited to the Women Leader's Network in New Zealand, and then I got caught up in the momentum: for instance, when my brother and I found that sick bird on the last night before I moved across the country and we finally talked about our parents' divorce. My list was endless. I couldn't stop writing about all the things I've learned, all the talents I've discovered, and all the elements of my health that I'm so very grateful for. I couldn't believe how I felt after working through this process and seeing my tangible assets in plain view. Not only did I feel a very real sense of worth, I was inspired by a sense of abundance and a feeling of "more."

With this process, comes a sense of pride in knowing that, regardless of the struggles, frustration, and even disappointments you might be feeling right now, your life has been filled with experiences, learning, and talents that are worth something—if not to anyone else, they're worth everything to you.

Do you want to live your worth? Do you want to give yourself a gift? Spend the time to pull out a piece of paper, divide it into six sections, and start writing. I know this Balance Sheet exercise looks too simple to be meaningful. I've also read books where I stopped at an exercise and thought, "I'll read through the material and then get back to it later," and inevitably, I never do it. But I swear to you this simple little Balance Sheet exercise will make all the difference—not only in how you think about your worth but in the way you *experience* it. Your commitment to create a Personal Balance Sheet will make a tremendous difference in your ability to create *more*.

Still thinking about skipping over this section? Here are a couple of things I've come to learn about worth that will help you to understand the importance of this process:

Worth Comes Through Experience.

It's not something anyone can give you or anything you can "think" into existence. Actually sinking your teeth into the process and taking the time to not only think through, but to physically build your Balance Sheet is an opportunity for you to "experience" your worth full on.

Most of Us Are Not Great Assessors of Our Worth.

You simply can't deny what's right there in front of you. This process will help you to lay it all out so you'll have difficulty denying all that you're worth. Afraid of what you're going to find? Scared that this process will undermine you and you'll find you're not all that you thought? Don't be. I promise that you have been underestimating all that you're worth. I have never, *ever* done this Balance Sheet process with anyone who has not come out the other side thinking, "Hmm . . . not bad!"

We look at those around us and assume they have "more."

More talent, more money, more confidence. I'm asking you to focus wholly and completely on you. I don't care if your brother has a Ph.D. or your best friend has won a Pulitzer prize, this process is focused on you and only you. No comparisons required.

We Have Short Memories.

List five of your major accomplishments from last year. Stumped? I'm not a psychologist and hence, I don't have a technical explanation for this, but I've met with enough women to know that we can conjure up our failures, mistakes, and the critical things people have said to us with crystal clarity. Our accomplishments, successes, and compliments on the other hand, are not so clear. If you keep the notes you create as you work through these next two chapters, you're going to have a physical reminder of all that worth—something you can refer back to on a regular basis.

YOUR TANGIBLES

Your education, unique experiences, talents, skills, relationships, and health all make up your tangible assets. These are the things that an employer, banker, mentor, or investor can see and feel. They differ from the intangible assets we'll assess in the next chapter in that they are the more *objective* elements of your worth—there is a standard assessment of their value. For example, a Doctorate in chemistry M.B.A. has a common value in the marketplace.

What comes next is a discussion of each of your tangible assets and some questions and challenges to help you get started. If you're going into this with a little trepidation, moving one foot at a time into the deep end, get a piece of paper and divide it into six sections, with Education, Unique Experiences, Talents, Skills, Relationships, and Health at the top of each. If you're ready to dive in, grab a pile of paper and let yourself go. And that's the key: Let yourself go. Don't just write down your Bachelor of Arts, write down key learning you've had on the job, and describe a failure that gave you a great big lesson from the "school of hard knocks."

As you move through this process, you'll naturally begin to look into the future. You'll start to think about "more." How can I further develop this talent? Who are the key people I need to meet in order to further build my relationship bank? Each and every one of these assets can be built upon. Consider how you can take each element of your worth to the next level.

Education

Twenty, forty, sixty thousand dollars later, good God, that diploma on your wall better be worth something! Whether you're still knee-deep in student debt to the government, the bank, or your parents, never, ever doubt this is money well spent. Your education is a tremendous asset; it's a legitimizing tool that helps others discern your value before they get to know your intangible attributes, and it's something that no one can take away from you.

That said, the real value of your education isn't in the diploma or the degree. It's in your willingness and ability to learn and apply your knowledge, an expanded view of the world, your ability to think critically, and the determination to sit down and write that paper when you really want to watch a movie. These are foundational learning tools that you cannot, and will not, be able to create success without. And education doesn't stop once you leave the classroom. The world of work is filled with both formal and informal opportunities to keep on learning.

Above all else, remember that education and more importantly, learning, is what you make it. And, if you don't have any letters after your name, don't worry. While you can't be a brain surgeon without slogging your way through medical school, there's a whole world of possibilities out there. If you want the credentials, go to school and get them. If not, don't ever use your lack of education as an excuse. You may very well be more qualified than the Harvard grad seated beside you.

> An investment in knowledge pays the best interest.
> —Benjamin Franklin

✳ strategy

Make a list of all your educational experiences and achievements—degrees, courses, lectures you've attended—and write down at least five key pieces of learning you took away from these experiences. Don't get writing, "I can list each level from Maslow's Pyramid of Needs" unless you really feel this knowledge impacts your worth in the marketplace.

TAKE-AWAY

One of the most influential bosses in my career required that I write down my "lessons learned" each and every week when I submitted my progress report. It turned out to be a critical tool in creating success.

Every week, write down at least five things that you've learned. It focuses your learning and more importantly, gives you a record to reflect upon. Really, there's nothing like reading back and realizing you've "learned" the same lesson ten times over.

NEXT STEPS

How has your education (or lack of) affected your career success?
Are there courses, diplomas, or degrees you need to accomplish your next series of goals, or does your learning need to take place in the marketplace?

Unique Experiences

A year off to travel the world in the midst of a thriving career may look like career suicide to some, but to my friend Lisa this was the opportunity of a lifetime. *Life* being the key. Sometimes we experience things in life that may not look like an asset to our career, but are a direct link to making it big. Don't believe me? Take it from Lisa:

> My travel experience has given me a perspective that is valuable to globally minded companies (which is just about every company) and it helped me hone skills such as my "ability to deal with stress" and "ability to deal with ambiguity"—qualifications you often see listed on job descriptions these days. The experience was wonderful. It built my confidence in my ability to tackle any challenge, and I would do it again in a second.

You spent a month in Africa studying endangered species. You're a classically trained pianist. You've been a Big Sister since you were twenty. Not only are these experiences impressive and unique, these tangible resources will also help you to build your intangible assets. Think about it. There's nothing like traveling through India to inspire compassion, for example. It doesn't matter what, exactly, you've done. What's important is what you've learned from it, and how your efforts have boosted your confidence. And boost it they should! It takes guts and determination to go beyond the simple school/work/more-work cycle.

> You are unique. If that is not fulfilled, then something has been lost.
>
> —Martha Graham

✳ strategy

What are the most unique experiences you've had? And remember my bird story. Write down the obvious experiences you're likely to tell anyone who will listen, but also those heartfelt experiences that have shaped the way you relate to others and yourself.

TAKE-AWAY

I just learned from one of my colleagues that she worked on Greenpeace campaigns and has traveled around the world. One of the biggest mistakes we make is thinking that no one cares about our lives outside of our work.

Find the opportunity to integrate your unique life experiences into conversations with bosses, clients, and investors. You might have similar stories that create lasting bonds, and they may also have great ideas about how you can integrate your transferable life skills into the workplace.

NEXT STEPS

Sometimes it's difficult to get your head around the concept of taking a sabbatical to write a book, traveling out of town to care for a family member, exploring the world—anything that could take you away from your thriving career. In reality, these experiences are what make you marketable. What are five things you need to experience before the end of your life? How can you create the time and space to live them?

Talents

Hear this. The quickest, surest, and most effective way to create wealth is to identify and work within the realm of your talents. Could Celine Dion have been a waitress? Could she have folded a killer T-shirt at the Gap? Could she have been an office manager? My guess is yes. But what ensures that Celine has more money than the Bellagio Casino is the fact that she has identified and built a career around her talent—her voice. We can all do a load of different things, but it's our talents—those unique, natural, soul-feeding assets—that bring home the bacon.

People pay for talent because, for the most part, it's unique. Why, if everyone has talent, is it so unique? Because there are way too many people out there who are slogging their way through their life denying, stifling, or ignoring their talents. The exploration and identification of talents is challenging, as it's often attached to something personal, and it requires us to give of ourselves in a way that makes us vulnerable. You have to ask yourself, is it worth it? Are you worth it?

Here's the most important thing you have to remember about your talents. Just because they come easily, the majority of us don't realize that our talent could be the basis of a thriving career. Yes, creating success and getting what you're worth requires effort, but no, the thing you *do* to create success does not, and quite frankly should not, be death-defyingly hard, boring, or unsatisfying. I've seen this with clients again and again. One of my past clients LOVED shopping. She fought me, tooth and nail, that she could not possibly turn that into a career. Two years later, she has one of the most successful celebrity shopping businesses in North America—can you imagine? And remember Claire and Cheyann, the C&C California T-shirt moguls we interviewed in the last chapter? These women knew very little about designing clothes, but man, did they love T-shirts. They loved everything about them—how they felt, how they aged, and how you could throw one on with everything from jeans to a bathing suit and feel fantastic. They just couldn't find a T-shirt on the market with that lived-in, comfy, actually-covers-your-belly-button feeling. So, they created their own.

Not only is C&C California a reflection

> Being a singer is a natural gift. It means I'm using to the highest degree possible the gift that God gave me to use. I'm happy with that.
>
> —Aretha Franklin

of Claire and Cheyann's love for T-shirts, it's a great example of translating your personal experiences—and your intuition about what other people will also love and pay for—into a satisfying career. Don't get stuck thinking that talents are all about singing, dancing, or having a great head for numbers. Talents are diverse and inherently interesting. What's your talent?

✳ strategy

Make a list of your talents. Photography, singing, dancing—break free from the traditional list. Are you naturally funny? Are you comfortable in front of a crowd? Are you a visionary? Do your plants thrive and bloom, while others struggle to keep a cactus alive? This is not the time to be modest. Don't think you have any talents? You do, and you're just scared. And you should be, looking at your talents is scary. Once you actually identify your talents, there is a very strong innate sense of responsibility and it hangs on until you do something about it. I guess you have to ask yourself, What's worse? The fear of revealing your talent, or the fear of keeping it locked up inside you?

TAKE-AWAY

Remember that even the most innate and natural of talents require practice, work, and discipline. Serena Williams is a naturally talented tennis player, but what makes her a champion? Her work ethic.

NEXT STEPS

Think about how you can take your talents to the next level. How can you enhance your natural gifts? Singing lessons? A wine course? Showing your architectural sketches to a trusted friend? Keep thinking.

Skills

I don't love budgeting, but I can do it. I don't love negotiating vendor contracts, but I can do it. I don't love accounting, but I can do it. These are the skills I've had to learn in order to build a business around my talents—writing and speaking.

I'm a big believer that we focus our careers, our talents, on what we enjoy and what comes naturally. But if talent is at the core of your investment, circling around your talent are your skills. These are things you may not love to do, but you're required to do in order to support and sustain your talents.

Yes, ideally you want to spend a solid 80 percent of your day focusing on your talents and delegate the things you don't necessarily enjoy doing to someone else. But in order to have a working knowledge of how your business or your job works in totality, you simply have to keep your feet wet. For example, I have an accountant, an investor who's an accountant, and an office manager who writes my checks—I've got my back covered. But (and this is a big but), when it comes down to it, *I'm* responsible. I sign the company checks, and it's up to me to understand where the money is coming from and where it's going.

While the real money is in your talent, your skills are incredibly valuable, especially if they complement your talents. For example, as a financial analyst,

> No one can arrive from being talented alone. Work transforms talent into genius.
>
> —Anna Pavlova

your talent is an understanding of numbers and how they work together to create a business case, but your skill is knowing how to input that information into a spreadsheet so other people can access it. Think about your skills as acquired assets. And just like your talents, you always want to increase your skill base. You may not love using computer spreadsheets to keep track of your freelance gigs, but taking a course and honing your skills will ensure you have more time to actually do the work and earn more money.

✱ strategy

Make a list all of your skills. These don't have to be the things you love, but the things that, when push comes to shove, you know how to do. You might never, ever want to be a stenographer or a typist, but your ability to type and type quickly is an asset in almost every field.

TAKE-AWAY

The world of work is in a constant state of flux and your skill base needs to be constantly improving. Take a look at industry magazines and websites and attend trade shows in order to keep up on emerging trends that may inform skills you'll need down the road.

NEXT STEPS

What skills are you lacking to take your talent to the next level? Who are the leaders in your field and what do they know how to do that you don't? Ask for an opportunity to speak to your boss, another business owner, or a "star" in your field. Ask how they developed their skill base and how they ensure they're always up to par.

Relationships
It's not what you know. It's who you know.

Like it or not, there's no truer statement in today's marketplace. The world today is all about relationships—who you know, how you know them, and why you're on their speed dial.

Personal relationships have eclipsed the whole resumé-and-application process. When most companies post job opportunities, they get

> Everyone has talent. What is rare is the courage to follow that talent to the dark place where it leads.
>
> —Erica Jong

absolutely flooded with applications. We're talking resumés by the thousands. But in times of shrinking budgets, the stakes are often too high to hire someone from two pages of high-quality-stock paper. Ninety-nine percent of the time, they've already got someone they know in mind; the credentials just seal the deal.

Personal relationships have also changed the whole process of building a business. If you're an entrepreneur and your business concept is too young or shaky, you may have to forego the traditional-lenders route and turn to your network. People don't tend to write checks to people they don't know, so, even if you're in the idea stage, get out there and start introducing yourself.

> I'm really lucky to be able to include the people I love on this crazy roller-coaster ride.
>
> —Mandy Moore

I have two primary investors in my business. They write me checks in return for equity in my business. But that's certainly not how it began. My investors were both mentors—intellectual investors—in my business for a full year prior to their cash injection. They were watching how I performed, assessing my integrity, and we worked together to build a foundation of mutual trust and respect. The relationship came first, and while yes, money changes the dynamic of any relationship, it's still just that—a relationship, and the stronger-and-longer, the better.

This idea of a relationship as a tangible asset might be a little confusing. Aren't relationships intangible? Here's the thing. Your ability to create relationships is an intangible attribute reliant on charisma, honesty, integrity—all of the characteristics we're going to discuss in the next chapter. But your relationships, your networks of friends, family, and associates, are one of the most important tangible assets you have going for you. If you want to increase your net worth, start with your network. Solid, respect-based relationships will help you achieve your dreams, and make the process infinitely more enjoyable.

✳ strategy

Make a list of your primary relationships. Think beyond your boss and the woman sitting in the office next to you. How about your cheerleaders—those people in your life that believe in, and support you? Do you have any corporate relationships you can leverage? For example, maybe you work for Citibank in New York and you want to transfer to the San Francisco office. Your "relationship" to the company will help you get the introductions you need.

TAKE-AWAY

Your relationships are of value to you but they are also of value to others. Think trade for a trade. Is there anyone you would like to meet who is known within your network of contacts? Is there anyone you can offer an introduction to, in exchange for an introduction or opportunity that you need?

NEXT STEPS

Be strategic. If you haven't already created a database of your network, do just that. Take a long look over it. Your relationships should always be expanding: Who do you need to know?

- -

Health

Here's the cold hard truth. I have a friend, John, who graduated as valedictorian of his M.B.A. program at one of the most prestigious schools in the country. Within weeks, his peers had all settled into incredible careers. John? He was still unemployed. Why, you ask? Because each and every time he sat down for an interview, the person across the desk was looking at a three-hundred-pound guy. Whether it was a fear that John was lazy, a heart attack risk, or maybe even the assumption that John has problems with feelings of worth, I'm not sure. What I am sure of is that John didn't get the job of his dreams because he's unhealthily overweight.

Without your health—mental and physical—your balance sheet is virtually worthless. Really, there's not much you can do from a hospital bed.

I know it's tough in the face of sixty-hour weeks to hit the gym every two days, but please, please know that if you don't take care of your body and mind, they can't take care of you. You don't need to be a triathlete in order to excel in the health category. This is about eating as well as you can (or at all), getting your heart rate up to a point in which you remember that you have one, and, on the mental front, taking the time to rest your mind.

Still don't believe that your health is a major commodity? If you want to make the big bucks, then get ready for a physical and/or a psychological assessment. In most corporations and even in order to get insurance as a business owner, you're going to have to provide a urine sample, undergo a blood test, and consent to a basic physical. Employers, investors, banks—they consider your health a commodity. How about you?

* strategy

How physically healthy are you? When was the last time you saw a doctor, exercised, ate a piece of lettuce? When was the last time you had a physical? List all of your physical accomplishments—you ran a 5K, you put the brakes on a growing Starbucks addiction, you quit smoking. If you're still at a loss on this one, write down every single thing that you are thankful for, as it relates to your health. You have legs to walk on, eyes to see with. You can take big breaths of air without pain. You have long, beautiful fingers that allow you to play the piano.

TAKE-AWAY

Still think your health has nothing to do with your career success? For a week, stick to your regular routine and keep a log of your productivity—what you've accomplished. The next week, commit to exercising at least three times and keep the same detailed log. You might be spending three or four hours less at the office, but just watch your productivity soar.

NEXT STEPS

The first time the company I worked for "requested" that I have a physical exam for insurance purposes, I was a bit perturbed. "Can they do that?" was my defensive question. "Yes," was the Human Resources manager's straight answer, "if you want to work here." I was actually a bit scared. I was twenty-seven and in the prime of my life. *There's nothing wrong with me . . . or is there?* I had more than a few sleepless nights conjuring up every ailment in the book. I panicked, thinking, *There is no way I want to find out I have Tourette's syndrome from the company nurse.* I hightailed it to my own doctor and had a physical *before* my physical. Your next step? If you haven't had a physical in the last few years, call your doctor.

I'm still stinging from my goal-accomplishing experience, but as gut-wrenching as it is, I know that it's been a gift. It's through the hole of disappointment that we really get a good hard look at what we really feel we're worth, and I can assure you it has nothing to do with running a successful business, publishing a book, negotiating with Ford, wearing Theory clothes, or even having everyone think that "you're living the dream."

I learned two critical things from my brush with success. One, accomplishment is nothing without a feeling of worth. Two, your tangible assets just scratch the surface. It's your intangibles, the assets that make you who you are, that build the real foundation of your worth.

wildly sophisticated icon

✳ Jeanine Lobell

Makeup artist and founder, Stila Cosmetics

Vision, imagination, and some of the coolest cosmetics on the planet. Jeanine Lobell is the mind behind Stila Cosmetics and a sought-after celebrity makeup artist. She's wielded her brushes on Hollywood beauties including Gwyneth Paltrow, Natalie Portman, Debra Messing, Cate Blanchett, Cameron Diaz, and Charlize Theron.

Born in Sweden and raised in Europe, Jeanine completed school in London, then moved to Los Angeles, where she launched her career by doing makeup for music videos. Next came magazine covers, high-profile clients, and plans for a new, more down-to-earth line of cosmetics.

Jeanine founded Stila in 1994, the same year she had her first child. Now, Stila is a major player in the cosmetics industry—known for its quirky, recycled packaging and some seriously innovative products. Estée Lauder acquired the Stila brand in 1999, but Jeanine remains the president and CFO, with full creative control. Jeanine is married to actor Anthony Edwards (from the television series *ER*), and the couple have four children under the age of ten.

What is the best investment you've ever made?
When people get to know me, they always say, "You know, you have the best people around you." Whether it's in my company or in my personal life, I really invest in my relationships. And that's a big reason why professionally, people have been with me nine years, and why I've had the same friends for fifteen to twenty years. There's something really grounding about keeping people around you for the majority of your lifetime, because they're going to tell you what you need to hear. Like, "Jeanine, you're totally full of shit!" Those are the people who will tell you. My relationships are very important to me—they're the best investment I've ever made.

What advice would you give to young women?

You really need to sit down and figure out what you want. That's the first thing. And are you doing what you want to do or are you doing what other people told you to do? You have to decide if you're on a path that you truly feel is yours. I can remember having lists when I was twenty years old—trying to figure out what I needed to do to put it all together. I'd think, "This is what I can do today to get me to the next place." You just have a list, and that's all you can do. And for some people it's three things, and for some people it's ten things, and for some people it's twelve things. You have to find out what's perfect for you, and then set out to achieving your lists—and that will get you on the right road.

How do you define your worth?

I think it's defined by who you are and who you bring into the world. And how you treat people. Your contributions to your personal relationships and the bigger picture. That is what makes you worthy.

What have you had to learn in order to get where you are today?

In the beginning, I didn't even know how to lay out an order form, or order labels, or manage inventory. I had to learn how to run sales and manage distribution, and just an enormous amount of stuff. But I think I was always able to say, "I don't know." And you know what? People respond really well to that. They're less interested in people who only pretend to know what they're saying. You have to be sort of egoless in order to learn.

What's your greatest achievement to date?

Having four incredible children and a lasting relationship. Every time I say that I have four kids, people always ask, "With the same man?" And I say, "Yeah." I guess that's not a strange question, after all.

3

What Am I *Really* Worth?

Discovering Your Intangibles

I can still see it clear as day. Four words that jumped off the resumé like a neon sign:

Enormous capacity for work.

Now, I don't love résumés. I tend (like most of the hiring population) to go on referral, but with limited time on my hands and a mountain of work on my desk, I found myself sifting through a mere 100 resumes searching for someone, *anyone,* who could help me organize my office, my business, and my life. I've been asked at least a thousand times what makes a great résumé, and while I'm happy to talk about the fundamental importance of ensuring its particular relevance to the audience and the need to keep it results-oriented—there's simply something else to it.

Yes, your education, your talents, and your experiences all play a role in your Balance Sheet, but time and time again, I've learned that the fundamental essence of building wealth comes down to the intangible.

Enormous capacity for work. I looked at those four words, picked up the phone, and arranged a meeting. Two days later, I hired Rox, my beloved office manager.

"I'm fiercely determined. I'm dedicated to seeing things through to fruition. I love to laugh." These are the intangible elements of worth that make up the very unique-to-you portion of your Balance Sheet. If you're still thinking "intangibles" are not concrete enough to truly create career success, think again. Just like fear, hunger, and love, you can't touch them, but that doesn't make them any less real. In fact, it's *because* you can't "touch" them and because your combination of intangible traits is unique to you, that these assets become all the more powerful. There are hundreds of thousands of people out there with an M.B.A. degree, but how many of them are loyal? Hopeful? Compassionate? If you want to increase your ability to earn—money, respect, influence—focus on your intangible attributes. These traits are the most treasured assets in the marketplace.

No, your intangible attributes may not come out in an interview, or even during your first week at work. But do know this: Whether in the face of dealing with a difficult client, or staying up all night to finish a particularly challenging proposal, or being asked to keep the confidence of your business partner—they will be revealed. You will have a myriad of opportunities to express your intangible attributes, especially if you consciously assess yourself and have a strong sense of which qualities you possess.

Here's a rundown of the top ten intangible assets you'll need to gain wealth, power, and influence. Think of these as a starting point. In reality, the list is endless—and extremely personal. Use these descriptions and questions to help you identify and explore the parts of yourself you might not regularly think of as business or money-making assets. Then use the applications to prove to yourself and to those around you that you're worth it!

The evaluation of your intangibles is a lot different from that of your tangibles. Your Rolodex, the degree hanging on your wall, and the photo album from your trip through Europe are all things you can touch and feel. Your intangibles are more difficult to assess. They require that you explore your behavior, your emotions, and your mannerisms with an open mind. The most important thing you need to be aware of in reading through the following section is that in 99.9 percent of cases, we underestimate ourselves. Your task here is to look at yourself more than objectively; you need to look at yourself abundantly.

After each description, I've laid out some questions that will get you thinking about each of these intangibles. The most meaningful way to get something through this process is to pull out a journal or turn on your computer and start writing your responses.

Just like our tangible assets, our intangibles can also be built upon. I've included a Next Steps challenge that will help you to build your sense of worth.

INTANGIBLES

Hope

It was a critical time in a company I was working for, and I opted to focus a team meeting on the concept of hope. Our director of operations, a former army commander, came into my office an hour afterward and said, a mere inch from my face, point-blank, "Hope is not a strategy." Thank good God I had just read a quote from Napoleon Bonaparte in preparation for the meeting and was able to come right back at him with the words of his idol: "Leaders are dealers in hope."

Hope is defined as "to desire with an expectation of obtainment." How often have you either failed or succeeded upon the power of your expectations? Hope is exactly what creates the foundation for success. Solutions, innovation, perseverance—these all come from hope. I disagree with my former army colleague. Hope is one of the most powerful strategies you have in your arsenal of worth. It's not only something you can build within yourself; it's also an extraordinary gift to share with others.

✳ strategy

Do you consider yourself hopeful?

Have you ever used hope as a strategy? **How did it make a difference?**

Have you ever lost your sense of hope? **How did it feel?**

If you were to look around a room of ten other people, how would you guess you rate in the hope department?

NEXT STEPS

I know a lot of young women who are afraid to hope. Afraid of being disappointed. But I want you to hope for something—really hope. I want you to let your mind go, to think about, dream about, and imagine what it would be like for your hope to come true. Each and every day for a month, write down your hope in all the glorious detail you can muster.

Listening

Hands down, your ability to listen is an extremely compelling asset. Not the kind of listening that says, "Yeah, yeah, I've got what you're saying, just wait until you hear what I have coming back at you", but rather, "Let me really hear you and concentrate on what you're saying so I can better understand."

Think about it. Your client's needs, your boss's expectations, your investor's concerns—the truest and most effective way of understanding, unraveling, and ultimately resolving comes through listening.

The benefits are twofold. The better we're able to listen, the more information we have access to, and let's be clear, information is power. Your clients, your boss, even your friends are telling you everything you need to know. I experienced this yet again the other day in a meeting.

We're in the midst of negotiating a deal with a blue-chip automotive company and the agency representative from Young & Rubicam interjected a story I initially thought had nothing to do with what we were talking about. Frustrated, another player in the room, someone from her own team, tried to cut her off and bring her back round to the discussion at hand. Thinking, "there's got to be something to this," I encouraged her to finish. In the end, she was telling us the story of a company that had overpromised and had made her look bad in the eyes of her client. What she was really telling us was that she'd been burned in the past, she was on thin ice with the client, and most importantly, that in order to get the deal, we needed to help her feel comfortable with solid examples of execution and delivery.

The other benefit of listening comes from the fact that most of us are not used to being heard—really heard—and when we encounter someone who we feel in our gut is truly committed to listening, we feel infinitely more connected. Listening is the key to building one of the most important tangible assets from the previous section: relationships.

A part of your listening repertoire includes your ability to ask questions—questions that elicit authentic, focused, and articulate responses. One of the things I was most afraid of when I started taping the television series I created and coproduced *Making It Big,* was the fact that I'm not a journalist and the show required I ask a lot of questions—in public! I've learned, through the show, that the best questions actually emerge when listening from your heart. Not forcing questions, trying to predecide what question to ask while you're listening, but trusting that, if you are really hearing, the questions will flow naturally.

One last thing. This intangible isn't just about listening to others; it's also about listening to yourself. There's a Cherokee staying that states "Listen to the whispers and you won't have to hear the screams." Have you ever noticed a little voice in the back of your mind telling you something you're not quite ready or willing to hear? After days, months, even years of ignoring the voice, it becomes louder, more pronounced, more distracting. Still not listening? Watch life start to scream. Your ability to hear the whisper will serve you equally well in your personal and in your professional life. Listen to others. Listen to yourself. Listening is the key to creating more.

* strategy

How well do you listen? **This is a question that may be difficult for you to answer objectively. Ask a close friend or colleague for her honest thoughts. Be willing to listen and really hear her response.**

Do you find that you generally ask questions that elicit the information you need?

Have you ever left a conversation that left you feeling understood? **What kind of questions did the person ask? How did they probe you in a way that allowed you to reveal yourself? Is there a technique they used that you could incorporate into your repertoire?**

Do you listen to yourself? **Do you trust your instincts?**

Have you ever heard a whispering you didn't respond to? **How did you feel? What were you afraid of hearing?**

NEXT STEPS

Start on a personal level rather than in a professional context (less threatening and potentially dangerous if you don't pull it off so well). Engage someone in a conversation. You probably have dozens of conversations each day, but approach this one a little differently. Allow yourself to really listen. Ask natural, spontaneous questions. Probe deeper. Focus on the other person rather than mentally planning your next question or comeback. If you find your mind wandering or you're fighting yourself not to interrupt, bring yourself back to the conversation and engage again. Listening skills can be built.

"How did that make you feel?" "What surprised you most about that situation?" "What can I do to help?"

You might be surprised at how willing even professional colleagues are to engage in answering seemingly personal lines of questioning, especially if they believe you will listen and seriously consider their responses.

Courage

In *Wildly Sophisticated: A Bold New Attitude for Career Success,* I suggest that courage is born when you can feel, see, hear, and taste fear . . . and you make the decision to leap anyway. The magic begins when we courageously leave what we've known to trust, and hope for something more.

There are two critical components of the courage equation—intuition and an ability to make decisions without knowing the outcome. I was reminded of this the other day over coffee as my new friend Maria told me about taking a leave from her amazing job as the New York bureau chief at *People* magazine on a gut feeling that she needed to try her hand at something different—without a clear sense of the eventual outcome.

> The moment somebody says "This is risky" is the moment it becomes attractive to me.
>
> —Kate Capshaw

"I'm an adventurer at heart. I love challenge and I love to learn. I've been thinking about writing fiction, I've applied for a writing fellowship, I could travel for the summer. I'm not sure what I'm going to do, but I'm compelled to try something different. It's tough. Everyone thinks I'm crazy to leave this amazing job, and I'm not entirely sure what I'm going to come back to find."

We often think courage is about climbing Everest or coming to the defense of an elderly woman who's had her purse snatched. In fact, courage is something you choose to live every single day. Courage is taking responsibility for something you're not exactly sure how to do. Courage is taking a stand and defending something you believe, even in the face of critics. Courage is telling the truth, even when it could get you in deep shit.

So why risk? We decide to take courageous action when the possible rewards—personal, financial, emotional, you name it—are worth leaping for. Courage requires a willingness to fall, to get back up, and to leap again. In life and work, courage and your use of courage to take risks is truly one of the most important qualities you can possess.

✳ strategy

Would you define yourself as courageous?

What is the most memorable thing you've ever done that required courage?

Have you ever been too courageous?

NEXT STEPS

Courage is relative, and you know yourself best. Choose something you've been thinking about doing or changing in your life. It's best if you have a gut feeling but you don't have a clue how it could turn out.
Now do it.

Compassion

Compassion is a very powerful and highly underrated career asset. I remember the very first time I ever gave a Wildly Sophisticated LIVE presentation to a group of graduating college students. Quite frankly, I was more afraid of this group of twenty-one-year-old, highly-coiffed, posturing, I've-got-it-all-together, what-can-you-tell-me-that-I-don't-already-know? young women than I had felt about presenting to the vice president of the United States. I came into the room, watched the students stream in, and wondered, "Why do I feel afraid?"

> You have not lived a perfect day, even though you have earned your money, unless you have done something for someone who will never be able to repay you.
>
> —Ruth Smeltzer

I thought back to my graduating class and imagined what we would have looked like, and remembered how we were all feeling—scared. I got into the mind-set of what it feels like to have invested in your college diploma, the pressure of your parents and friends asking, "So what are you doing after graduation?" the sneak peeks at the newspaper talking endlessly about the unemployment rate, the feeling like, "Do I have to choose the career for the rest of my life now?" and I was overcome with empathy. It is scary. I walked down the stairs of the auditorium to the podium and with a breath of compassion, I shared everything I remember feeling that I didn't know, but that no one seemed able to tell me. That presentation, based upon a feeling of utter compassion, took me away from the fear of my own failure to thinking calmly and compassionately about how I could make life easier for these women.

If you're a teacher, saleswoman, CEO, social worker, actor, regardless of what you do, if you can find the compassion—the "Why am I doing this, what purpose does this serve, how am I making life easier or better for someone else?"—you will be worth more.

We can't talk about compassion for others without exploring compassion for ourselves. You need to take care of yourself in order to take care of others.

How often are you easier on your friends, family, colleagues, and staff than you are on yourself? *"Take the afternoon off." "Don't worry about those dishes. I'll wash up." "That's an easy thing to miss, don't beat yourself up."* Your ability to nourish, support, and take care of yourself directly corresponds to your ability to provide these things for others.

And *others* are the key to your success. You need to take care of yourself in order to identify who around you needs your compassion. Compassion ranges from spending extra time to show that new intern the ropes and taking her to lunch on her first day, to committing your new business to a community cause you believe in. No one's going to ask if you're compassionate midway through a job interview. But compassion will set you apart from the pack, build strong relationships, and more than anything, it will keep you from straying from your values and your instincts. Your compassion is worth millions.

✳ strategy

Do you believe in what you do? How does it make a difference to the lives of others?

Do you have compassion for your "customer/client"?

What stirs your heart? An elderly woman struggling to cross the street? A lost dog? A woman packing up her kids to leave an abusive relationship? We all have our own causes or issues we feel passionate about, and they often come from our personal experiences.

Are you harder on yourself or others?

When was the last time you were compassionate toward yourself? What did you do for yourself?

When was the last time you helped someone else when it was absolutely inconvenient for you to do so?

NEXT STEPS
At the core of compassion is a desire to be helpful for the sake of being helpful, not to impress others. Do something compassionate for someone without that person or anyone else knowing that you've done it.

Charisma

Have you ever witnessed someone so awkward, so uncomfortable in her own skin, so unable to express herself naturally that it actually hurts to watch? There's a part of you that wants to jump in and intervene. I swear, you almost don't know how important charisma is until you encounter someone who lacks it.

In consulting with a woman who needed "charisma-building" help, her fear was that it was based purely upon personality, something so inherent it can't be defined or altered, and that charisma-building was only something that comes packaged as a smarmy laugh and exaggerated hand gestures.

This is not true on either front.

First and foremost, you can build charisma. But it's not about trying to be someone else; it's about being the most authentic version of yourself. It sounds ridiculously simple and slightly reminiscent of childhood picture books, but the best way of building charisma is to "be yourself." You can also think about the people you'd call charismatic. What have they got? A love of life, a passion, an ability to truly get past themselves and engage with others, an ability to look someone in the eyes, an easy laugh, a willingness to share of themselves. We're drawn to people who instantly make us feel at ease. And you can't make someone else feel at ease if you're not. Charisma is all about being the best of yourself regardless of what that is—mysterious, outspoken, shy, gentle, gregarious.

And this leads to the fact that so often we confuse charisma with extroversion, but they're not the same thing. You don't have to be the life of the party to have charisma. It can be quiet and subtle—think Sarah McLachlan, Gwyneth Paltrow, or Johnny Depp. Charisma simply means you're comfortable in your own skin, and you transfer that feeling to the people around you.

> What probably confuses people is that they know a lot about me, but it quite pleases me that there's more they don't know.
>
> —Bjork

Charisma is a critical component of being able to sell, and selling is a critical component of leveraging for more—more money, more respect, more influence—in your career and in your business. People "buy" from people they like, people they feel comfortable with—people with charisma!

✳ strategy

Do you consider yourself charismatic?

When have you used charisma to your advantage?

How is flirting different from charisma? Is it easier for you to have charisma in your personal life or in your professional life? How is it different?

What parts of your personality, your life, and your spirit could you share more openly with other people?

NEXT STEPS

With fear of sounding redundant, being charismatic is all about being yourself. Well, who the hell are you? The second chapter of *Wildly Sophisticated: A Bold New Approach to Career Success* is called "Who Do You Think You Are?" This is a critical question to ask yourself in creating more in your life and your career. After you've completed both your assessment of tangible and intangible worth, take some time to really think through and reflect on your answers. Ask yourself, "Who do I think I am?" and consider bringing "more" of you to your professional life. You might be surprised by what you get back.

Integrity

The core of integrity is truth. Your ability to express truth and integrity in *all* aspects of your life is the surest indicator of how intrinsically worthy you feel. You need truth to act on your intuition (to be able to hear your truth), to build intimate relationships (to be able to reveal your truth), and to express your passions (to be able to live your truth).

I've seen the importance of integrity time and time again and it's been inspiration enough to build more. In the height of the Internet bubble, everyone and anyone had a new venture and more money than they could spend. On my first day as managing director of an online gift-giving company, I was told quite literally, "We never use the word profit and this will be an exercise in spending money." I should have been infinitely more suspicious than I was (or perhaps more truthfully, I was suspicious, but wanted the opportunity, and didn't want to see the reality).

To make a long story short, this business was not at all what it was made out to be and there were a number of people involved who had no integrity—and others who did have integrity. As the business crumbled, those without integrity were laid off and are still unemployed three years later—no one will touch them. Those with integrity found opportunity within days of the closure.

Enron is an even clearer example. Who would you hire? Former company CEO Ken Lay or Sherron Watkins, the woman who had enough integrity and courage enough to tell the truth?

Integrity and worth have this wonderfully reciprocal nature. Acting with integrity is the surest way of increasing your sense of worth, and the more worthy you feel, the greater your ability to act with integrity. Integrity is the consistency and the manner with which you exercise your compassion and uphold your own standards; it makes you reliable and it inherently commands respect. When people know they can rely on you to tell the truth, to be loyal, and, simply put, to take the high road, you become priceless.

> It's my experience that you really can't lose when you try the truth.
>
> —Sharon Stone

✳ strategy

What does integrity mean to you? **Would you put yourself in that category?**

Have you ever worked in a situation that just felt wrong? **Or one that you knew was wrong? How did it affect your sense of worth?**

Do you always tell the truth? **Is lying ever acceptable? In what circumstances have you lied?**

NEXT STEPS

Perhaps you always, always tell the truth, but if there's something you've been hiding—whether it's to protect your own ass or another's feelings—resolve to tell the truth, the whole truth, and nothing but the truth, and enjoy the freedom, respect, and calm that comes from the process.

Graciousness

Oh my God. I'm sitting on a plane after learning a huge lesson about being gracious. I wish I could feel differently but I don't; maybe it's my lack of graciousness. Back in the terminal I had caught the eye of two women I had just introduced to my literary agent in New York. I walked toward them.

> "How did the meeting go?"
> "Great. We're going to submit a proposal next week."
> "Congratulations."

"Yeah."

Silence.

Here's what I should have said to them. "When someone offers you support, help, introductions, even if they don't expect thanks, they sure as hell notice when it doesn't materialize."

Being gracious is also being interested in the lives of others. It's about the Wildly Sophisticated philosophy of Getting Over Yourself. It again comes back to these same women. We have a makeup artist and hair stylist in common, and I learned just recently that in the three years of up-close-and-personal hair-and-makeup time together, neither one of them has ever, ever asked a personal question of this woman.

Graciousness is not just about saying thank you. It's about being thankful. It's about being able to comfortably accept both a compliment and criticism. It's about having compassion for others and a willingness to extend yourself. In this world of push, push, push, graciousness is a valuable attribute that will be greatly rewarded.

✳ strategy

Would you describe yourself as gracious?

Do you know someone whom you'd describe as being gracious? What inspires you to define her as gracious?

Are you authentically interested in the lives of those you work with?

NEXT STEPS

Grab a good pen, some heavyweight paper, and get ready to write some notes. Thank-you notes. It will take only minutes to think up a mere ten people you could extend a word of thanks or appreciation

to. In this age of e-mail and voicemail, taking the time to sit down and actually compose your thoughts on paper is a gift, and a gracious act that is not soon forgotten.

- -

Patience

It happens to the best of us. Maybe it's after college. Maybe it's after you knock the socks off your first boss and bound into a promotion. After you feel like you've got the lay of the land and you're in a full sprint toward success. Or once you've launched your new business. You hit a plateau of sorts. The next step? It takes longer than you expected. You start to wonder if you've lost your touch. You wonder if this is what you want to do anyway. You wonder if you're ever going to get to the next phase. You wonder why you can't get it into gear. It comes in all shapes and sizes, but for the majority of us, we hit a wall and the challenge is clear: to have patience.

I remember the first day I ever went over to the home of my best friend, Jenn. I was immediately struck by the fact that she had the *TV Guide* front page with a picture of an Oscar taped to her wall. Watching me stare just a moment too long, she offered, "I'm going to win an Oscar one day." That was almost twenty years ago and I believe her today the same way I believed her back then in her parents' home. Not once has she ever wavered from her vision. Is she sometimes frustrated, deflated, irritated, dejected? Of course. But she understands that, not only will this goal take time and patience, but she's also clear that on the journey to success, the way to sustain a sense of patience is to celebrate along the way.

Early in my career, I never would have guessed that patience is a true defining characteristic, but it is. Here's the truth: people tend to quit too early. In today's driving world of business, instant gratification is the name of the game, and we've become accustomed to seeing results—now. This is completely incongruent with the fact that success—big success—takes time and a willingness to persevere. If you have big aspirations, get ready for the long haul. Your ability to find the balance between initiative and patience is worth more than you can ever, ever imagine.

✳ strategy

Are you more naturally patient or impatient?

When have you had to be most patient?

What is the hardest part of being patient for you?

When you've been patient, where did you find the faith to sit still?

When has your patience been most tested?

NEXT STEPS

Patience is definitely not my strongest suit. But what I've learned is that it's something you can grow. It's something that becomes easier with time and practice. If you're questioning whether you've committed your full effort toward reaching a goal, make a list of everything you've completed and accomplished. When you're satisfied that you've done everything in your power, say a little prayer, and know it's in good hands. And please remember, surrendering is not the same as quitting.

Competence

"What do you actually want to get from your work?"

Surprisingly, most people don't know how to answer this question beyond "a paycheck." But over drinks one evening, my friend Challa put it this way. "You know," she said slowly, "I need to feel like I can actually do what I have to do. I need to feel like I have something to offer, that I'm good at something. I guess I need to feel competent."

This is huge, for a couple of different reasons. Who's kidding who? Of course we enjoy feeling as if we're good at what we do. Feeling competent actually builds confidence, confidence builds your ability to risk, and risk prepares you to try new things and build competence in more areas of your career or your business.

While your own feelings of competence are worth a tremendous amount, equally valuable is the faith others have in your level of competence. One of my business partners was talking with me about the components of partnership the other day. He believes there are three pieces to the puzzle: common goals, integrity, and competence. At first I was a bit surprised. "Competence—what do you mean?" His explanation? "I need to believe that, as your partner, when faced with a similar situation, with the same information, I would have made the same decision or done the same thing. I need to believe you are competent."

In short, the people you work with need to have confidence that you can get the job done. Competence is created with high standards, and by continually challenging yourself to improve.

* strategy

Do you feel competent in your current job or business?

What are your core competencies—what are you best at?

Have you ever been rewarded for your competence?

Do you feel as if you have the adequate talents, skills, and knowledge to succeed in your career or your industry?

We've had an intern in our office over the last few months, and at the end of her term, feeling that she hadn't met our expectations, it was time for a talk. We had agreed at the beginning of the partnership that she would regularly report her progress. Weeks later nothing had arrived. When asked what was going on, she said that she thought her accomplishments were obvious, and she didn't want to appear to be bragging.

A big part of ensuring others know that you're competent is ensuring that your competence is right there in front of them. Prepare reports, talk about what you're learning and accomplishing. Share your successes. Otherwise, how will people ever know?

Dignity

There are so many great lines in the film *The Contender,* but my favorite is when Joan Allen's character, Laine Hansen, pushed to respond to the allegations of sexual indiscretion, responds, "It is simply beneath my dignity." Dignity, self-respect, pride—call it what you will. Dignity has a funny way of protecting us. If we listen to our instincts, when our dignity is being jeopardized, we can't help but feel the call.

Dignity is about having standards for yourself—how you express yourself, how you demand to be treated, and how you decide to treat others. In this age of Britney Spears's bare midriff and Jerry Springer catfights, dignity is seemingly a lost art. This is a wonderful opportunity for you. Differentiate yourself by earning influence with an air of sophistication and decorum.

> I want things to be the best they can be. I want greatness.
>
> —Demi Moore

Many people are surprised to learn that having dignity and using it to create standards is actually one of the most significant of our intangible assets. "Doesn't my unwillingness to flirt with my boss make me less marketable?" Here's the reality. People respect, hire, trust, and pay for those who exhibit dignity toward themselves and others.

> I may be revered or defamed and decried; but I tried to live my life right.
> —Tracy Chapman

* strategy

What does dignity mean to you? Dignity is a word that's not bandied about all that frequently.

When have you acted with dignity?

Have you ever acted in an undignified manner? How did it make you feel?

NEXT STEPS

Without question, sometimes you need to move right past a boundary or a personal standard to realize it's there, but that said, thinking ahead through common (and even some uncommon) scenarios can help you understand where your lines of dignity begin and end.

BUILDING YOUR PERSONAL SENSE OF WORTH

A couple of years ago, I was watching a surprise birthday video almost six months after the actual event and I couldn't believe my ears. Jenn had a video camera and was asking my family and friends to describe me. I was hoping for "fun," "generous," maybe even "kind." Nope, each and every guest in that room offered adjectives around one theme, and one theme only—ambition. When I started out in my career and even in my business, I was driven by a very powerful and often very effective motivation.

My motivation? To prove that I could be successful. "I'll show you," became my mantra. It kept me up working late into the night, ensured that I didn't take holidays, and kept me in a limbo land between a real sense of worthiness and a true assessment of my own value. I was moving full speed ahead, trying to outrun my fear, and hoping one day I would prove to someone, anyone, that I'd made it.

What I've come to learn and what I can't make clear enough is that getting *more* requires that you feel like *more*. And no one else can give that to you. In order to create success on your own terms, you need a solid sense of worth without needing to show anyone, without it being attached to a dollar figure, or without it being contingent on obtaining the "big goal," whatever that is for you. You are worthy right here, right now.

Through this process of examining your tangible and intangible assets, I'm hopeful that you will see your worth with fresh eyes. But know that if, after assessing your assets, you're still not where you want to be, your worth is a work in progress.

There are some critical elements of worth that you need to understand:

Worth Is Not Static.

I don't know anyone who wakes up each and every day feeling exactly the same degree of "worthy." While the goal is to have a solid sense of worthiness that is not attached to anything but just being you, you, you, the reality is, we need to be prepared for our feelings of worthiness to ebb and flow. Don't be afraid of the day-to-day changes.

Worthiness Will Be Affected.

While perhaps the Dalai Lama lives with an unshakable and intrinsic sense of worthiness, for most of us, it's affected by others. One of the most important things you can do is to surround yourself with people who think you are as worthy as you do.

Worth Can Be Grown.

Here's the best part. You can grow your sense of worth. You have control. I had a surprising conversation with an acquaintance the other day that went from "We've had some great weather this month" to the plight of human suffering. His estimation? Suffering comes when our actions, our environment, our lives are inconsistent with what's in our heart. This sentiment sheds light on feelings of worth. The quickest way to nurture and grow a sense of worth is to follow your heart and your instincts—to tell the truth to yourself and others, and to do what you think is right.

> It isn't where you came from, it's where you're going that counts.
>
> —Ella Fitzgerald

Use What You've Got

Your past is what it is. Your family is who they are. Use what you've got. Some of the most successful people in the world have a drive that comes from some combination of sadness, anger, fear, or hurt. What they've learned is how to harness it—how to make it work for them, instead of against them. You can do the same.

Ask for Help

Depending on how tough your life experiences have been, and on your ability to objectively help yourself, you just might need professional help. Worth is a very personal, very sensitive, very complicated issue and not something that is easily "fixed." If you need help, get it. It's a sign of strength, not weakness.

Find a Passion

This is going to sound a little hokey, but I thank my passion for my career each and every day. When I first started to build my business, there were some days when I believed in it more than I did in myself. I actually used my passion for my business to build a sense of worth by creating standards, discipline, and a level of commitment that ensured that I would create success.

Find a passion that compels you to act in ways that are true to your character and reflective of what you really believe you are worth. I've had clients who have pursued their dreams because they wanted to show their child what is possible. Some clients have been so compelled to see the world, they hightailed their career in order to save the cash necessary to roam the globe. Other clients believed in the lives of people with AIDS and wouldn't stop until they made a difference. At some point, it has to extend beyond the passion for another person or thing and land back at you, but passion can be used as a very powerful catalyst to grow your worth.

Take Stock

Think about what your past has given you: strength, determination, love, resilience, respect—whatever. Whether you've come from a place of abundance and worth, or you've had major obstacles to overcome, as you've learned through these past two chapters, you have an arsenal of tangible and intangible assets that are yours and yours alone. Feel good about what you've got, and think about how you can capitalize on your past to build success beyond your wildest dreams.

I thank my lucky stars for "Enormous capacity for work." Without it, I don't know if I ever would have met Rox.

I've been thinking a lot about luck in relation to intangible assets. On some level there is something about the serendipity of finding the "right" person, reading the "right" sentence, receiving the "right" thank-you letter, or being asked the "right" question that has something to do with luck. But here's the thing. I was lucky.

Rox, she was smart.

Leaving this chapter, I want you to be clear about two things. First, your worth lives in the intangibles that, while you might not be able to see and feel them, are very real, very buildable, and very valuable. Second, you make your own luck. If I hadn't read and picked up this résumé, someone else would have.

If you grow your sense of intangible worth and develop these assets, I promise, you are going to find your more. Why? Because people will be lucky to have you.

wildly sophisticated icon

✳ Leila Josefowicz

Classical violinist

This is one woman who knows the meaning of commitment. Leila first picked up the violin when she was three, and made her Carnegie Hall debut thirteen years later at age sixteen. A decade later, Leila is one of the world's most recognized violin soloists.

After graduating from the renowned Curtis Institute of Music in Philadelphia, Leila has been busy traveling and playing across Europe, North America, and Asia. She has performed with some of the world's most prestigious symphonies, and has appeared on *The Tonight Show, Evening at Pops,* the BBC, and *Live from Lincoln Center* on PBS. Leila's expressive, virtuostic style can also be heard on a large collection of solo recordings.

In addition to a hectic schedule, the discipline of her profession, and constant travel, Leila has a four-year-old son named Lukas.

What's the most important lesson you've learned about money?
I think it's really important to be independent, financially speaking. If you can, resist the great generous donations of your boyfriend or your parents; it gives you a real sense of strength. Then, when you get to a more comfortable stage, you can say, "Hey, I did this on my own." And if you're not at that comfortable stage yet, at least you don't owe anybody anything. And that's a great feeling.

What has been the most surprising part of your career?

A lot of classical musicians are not socially savvy, which is a really interesting point. Because, between players, or between conductors or a soloist, or between a conductor and orchestral musicians, it's all about chemistry. You can't make great music with people if you're not enjoying their company to a certain degree. For example, there's no doubt that the conductor is leading the orchestra, but there has to be a certain type of charisma and pull for someone to be up there directing and having people enjoy their leadership.

What role does image play in your career?

I've had a little of the glamour thing going on for my record covers, but it's never been over the top. It's a fine line. You've got to try and get people's attention, but it has to be natural. You have to ensure that it's really you, because impressions are so important. If you're meeting a conductor, a potential boss—whoever—it's hard for people to shake certain impressions.

How do you define success?

I'm reaching a point in my career where I'm established in a different way. Where the music world really knows who I am, and they don't say, "Oh yeah, maybe I've heard about her." It's the stage where people really know you, and they know what to expect from you. A lot of classical music is proving yourself, over and over again. And when people go to hear you play, they're going as much to hear your personality as they are to hear the music.

4

What's My More?

Defining Your Values

It was a feeling that would begin to come over me Sunday night. A sense of disappointment. My energy would flag and regardless of how tired I was, I just couldn't get a restful night's sleep.

Monday morning I'd drive to work halfway wishing I'd get pulled over by an officer for speeding, except I was only going ten miles an hour, hoping never to actually arrive at the office. I'd wonder if this was just a persistent year-long flu bug that only hit on the weekdays. My coworker's laments about maternity leave with incessantly crying kids and no lunch break sounded luxurious.

I wasn't sure what would make me feel happy, only that I wasn't anywhere near satsified.

I wanted more.

can't even begin to count the number of young women I know who are dissatisfied in their careers, but they don't have a clue what will actually make them happy. What's more, they don't know what's making them *unhappy*.

Maybe you're finally paying the rent. You've got something that resembles a job, and perhaps even a budding career. You know you're destined for the corner office or you'll see your name in lights one day. But if you've been staring down the clock each afternoon and thinking, "There's got to be something more," then I promise you this—there is. The compulsion to shake things up, to reach for something bigger, to dream for something better means your life isn't working quite right. You've got a nagging sense that there's something else for you. Or, maybe that quiet voice in your head is getting louder: *"I don't want to go to work. I don't like who I am when I'm there. I don't like the people I spend my day with . . ."*

The desire to reach for more only gets more insistent if you ignore it. It gnaws at you until finally, you can't stay stuck. You have to take a risk. You start to focus on what's wrong and you have no choice but to take action— to make it right.

You're ready for more.

You wouldn't have picked up this book if you were infinitely satisfied— if you didn't want more out of your career. I believe that you can get anything you want. You just need to know what that *anything* is. This is the piece that most of us miss. We don't take the time to truly identify what it is that we want out of our careers. It's not that most people don't work hard, and that they don't have dreams and ambitions. It's that they haven't sat down and truly examined what they value and why they're spending 70 percent of their waking life on the job (or traveling to and from it).

What do I want? This isn't a selfish question. It's not a luxury, it's not ungrateful, it's not self-indulgent—it's essential. This is the question that lays the foundation for success.

The more you take from your career, the more you take from your business and your professional risks, the more you'll have to give. So often, people start selling—themselves, their services, their ideas—without knowing what they want in return.

In the last two chapters, you've honestly and abundantly assessed your worth—the innate experiences, talents, and attributes that no one can take away from you. You have everything you need to build a life that inspires and challenges you. And the more worthy you feel, the more likely you are to go after what you value, what you want. If you value yourself, you're going to transfer that strength into the world of work. Really, after you've spent a few hours listing all the amazing things you've done, survived, accomplished, and made of yourself, you're a lot less likely to take the crap your crazy coworker is dishing out. Understanding your worth defines what you're willing to tolerate, and what's simply not acceptable.

In this chapter, you'll use the solid sense of worth you built in the previous sections to move forward and figure out what you want from your career. From time, to freedom, to challenge, everyone will have a different answer and their own unique blend of priorities. You'll also fill out a detailed exercise that will help you identify your values, even if they don't feel clear from the start. When you know innately what

> Trust in what you love, continue to do it, and it will take you where you need to go.
> —Natalie Goldberg

you want, you'll be on the road to more wealth and more satisfaction. *More* of whatever you're looking for in the world of work.

WHAT DO YOU WANT?

Killer abs, a Louis Vuitton purse, a vacation in the tropics, world peace—don't we all? This section looks at what you want to get out of your *career*. When asked this question, one client responded, straight-faced, "a husband," but my guess is that you're looking for a little something more than a mate on the job.

The single best way to earn and to save more money is to live the life you desire. In return, money becomes a tool to build and achieve your dreams—not an empty pursuit. You can't separate your money from your work and expect to feel satisfied. You've got to know what else you want.

There are six primary "rewards" that the majority of us want to take from our work. Time, challenge, relationships, status, passion, money—everyone is working for one or some combination of these values. There are three things you need to consider as you read through the following descriptions and rate your values later in this section.

- **Be honest with yourself.** Your values end up dictating your choices and ultimately your reality—whether you like it or not. Britney Spears could tell you her primary value isn't profile, but after her famous kiss with Madonna, and her impromptu marriage and subsequent annulment, I'd be willing to make a hefty wager it's definitely on the top of her list. No judgment here, but the more honest you are with yourself, the more directly and strategically you'll be able to attain your "more."

- **Understand that your values are dynamic and interrelated.** Your values will not only change over time, but when examining these values in relation to each other, one might take priority over the other—depending on the circumstance. Your values are also interrelated. A focus on challenge and passion, for example, will directly feed your ability to make more money.

- **Know that your long-term values may require short-term choices.** While your primary value may be money, you may find a low-paying opportunity that allows you to learn and create relationships that, a year later, will pay off financially.

Time

Across the board, I've learned that time is the primary commodity young women are trading in. Sixty-hour work weeks have become the norm, the ticktock of biological clocks have inspired lightning-speed corporate ascents, and, in a world of midnight work sessions, wouldn't it be great if that morning coffee could be delivered through an IV drip?

I have clients who've taken demotions in order to train for an Ironman triathlon, and others who work day and night in start-ups, betting on retirement at forty. Time is one of the most important values you need to assess in your career. From how much of it you're willing to give, to how much flexibility you require, time is one of the most important values you've got. There are two primary elements of time that will help you realize both what you're getting into and what you want to get out of your time at work.

Don't Kid Yourself

You want to become partner at a top law firm? Get ready to spend some quality time with the cleaning staff. Long hours are a built-in function of the job and the corporate culture. If working around the clock in the same place makes you twitch, you will inherently be at odds with your own values. Not a great formula for success.

On the other hand, I have a friend who very consciously pursued a career in dentistry because the hours are limited and predictable (a fact I'm reminded of every time I try to book an appointment with *my* dentist—there's something strange about choosing a date in August when you're still in February), and she can pick her kids up from school by 3 P.M. She considered other forms of medicine, but dentistry was the best fit with her talents and her interests—and her desire to have a family. She values time with her kids and a job that doesn't involve late nights at her desk with an order of Mu Shu Pork.

Know that there will inevitably be days when you have to work longer and harder than usual, or times when you're giving more of yourself to your career. But each industry, position, and job title has its own unique relationship with the clock. If you understand these nuances before you dive in, you'll avoid any major surprises, and you can actually create work that fits your life.

Know Who's in Control

When I was in university, I paid my tuition by working at a paint factory through the summer. At exactly 10 A.M., a bell would ring to signal the first morning break. The same shrill alarm dictated our lunch and afternoon breaks. There's nothing like trying to slip in a last hand of rummy before you hit the conveyer belt again. By the end of the summer, I made a promise to myself: Never again would my time be dictated by the sound of a bell.

Time control isn't always this extreme, and in reality, even the president of the United States doesn't have full control over his schedule. There are realities of work—meetings, deadlines, shifts—that everyone has to deal with in their own way. Some people appreciate a predictable schedule and enjoy knowing exactly when their day will begin and end. Others chafe at a regimented routine and prefer to set their own schedule—they'll work at their own pace, and given their freedom, they'll finish the project on deadline. Thinking about how you value time and applying that understanding to your work will make the process infinitely more enjoyable, and ultimately, more successful.

We've all heard the expression, "time is money." Pretty cliché, right? I thought so too, until I heard someone use this old standby in a meeting a few weeks ago. I started to rethink it. When you're building "more," your time is a direct link to obtaining your desires. If your work requires a schedule that goes against your natural rhythms, it's going to have a huge impact on your sense of joy, passion, and accomplishment.

For example, I'm a morning person. I love waking up when the city's still quiet, and I do my best thinking before lunch. I'd make a terrible party planner, because I'd be snoozing in the foie gras by eleven. For me, the hours between six and twelve in the morning are literally my moneymaking hours. I think more clearly, I'm more optimistic, and I get about three times as much done before the midday slump begins. Over the years, I've learned how to capitalize on my early-morning energy. I try to schedule afternoon meetings. I don't answer the phone. I do whatever it takes to make the most of my own natural sense of time. I've also built a career that gives me control over my time, because I know that's equally important to me. Time *is* money. There's no question.

Where Do You Want to Spend Your Time?

This one may seem obvious, but trust me, it's not. I have a friend who trained to be an elementary school teacher. She liked kids, but she especially loved the challenge of watching them learn and grow. There was just one problem. She forgot that her work would keep her in a classroom all day—a classroom with paper cutouts, sandboxes and chalkboards. The other teachers (i.e., adults) gathered in the staff room at lunchtime, but once that bell had rung, it was just her and a room full of six-year-olds. After three years surrounded by finger paint and tiny coat hooks, she needed to start fresh.

As we build our careers and capitalize on our talents, interests, and skills, so many of us forget to think about *where* we'll be spending our days—a small point that has major implications for how you feel about your work. Are you willing to endure a long commute? Can you work in a big, open, noisy office or do you need a quiet space? Are you most comfortable on the sales floor of a chic department store or on a hiking trail for Outward Bound?

It's the final element you've got to consider: Where do you want to spend your time? In my experience, this little detail can help pinpoint your values with lightning speed. Why? It's so concrete that you get right into the daily reality of your work—the people, places, and things that define your job description.

CHALLENGE AND LEARNING

This is an important value for Wildly Sophisticated women. Why else did you work for that senator without pay or take a yearlong internship? Learning is a great reason to accept a job or tackle a new assignment. Really, this is what work's all about. The lessons you learn from one opportunity can be your gateway to something bigger, better, and more satisfying. How do you think Bill Gates made his way from computer geek to multibillionaire? I'm going to guess he didn't come out of the womb ready to build the world's biggest software company.

How important is learning to you? How important is it to feel challenged? Do you want a job where you're comfortable that you "know the ropes," or one where you're faced with a new situation (and new problems!) every day? These are important questions to ask yourself.

While challenge is the key to advancement and creating more, the reality is there are times when things in our personal life require our attention and absolutely necessitate a stress-free, challenge-free professional focus. Be realistic. If you just broke up with a long-term boyfriend, you've been battling a serious illness, or you're going through some tough personal or family issues, this is not the time to take on something big. Gather your strength first. You want to set yourself up for success, and you'll be far more likely to succeed if you have a clear head and a strong sense of focus.

This value can also be a bit tricky for the thousands of young women who are working in a job that is actually preparing them for something else. You need to understand that there are different "levels" of challenge in the world of work. Your current PR job may not be testing your limits, but maybe you're gathering contacts, experience, and skills for the day when you strike out and start your own firm. Your day-to-day "challenge level" may not be high right now, but it's preparing you for a major challenge down the road.

This scenario can also work in reverse. If you're swamped with stress and crazy everyday problems in a job that doesn't mean much to you, this can actually be a way of distracting yourself from building more—from taking on a challenge that's inherently meaningful, passionate and exciting.

I worked through the assessment tool you're going to encounter at the end of this chapter with a treasured employee. Her stated value for challenge is as high as it gets, and initially she wanted to indicate that her work with me at Wildly Sophisticated Media was totally meeting her needs.

> I've always loved a challenge.
>
> —Lana Turner

After thinking about it for a bit, she realized that her current role, while challenging, is not what she's *really* after in the long term. Her primary risk, or challenge, is to create her own business someday. We can keep ourselves in challenging or consuming jobs in order to avoid a more authentic challenge or to live out our dream career. Keep your challenge and learning focused.

Challenge, learning, moving beyond what you know right now—these are incredible returns from the investment you make in your work. When work makes your heart beat a little faster and gets the hairs on the back of your neck to rise, you know you're heading somewhere good.

RELATIONSHIPS

The pay is low. The hours are long. But you'll be working three doors down from the most innovative, inspiring woman in your industry. Even better, she'll be leading your weekly staff meeting. She works with an open door and encourages her team to keep her in the loop on all their projects. Suddenly, the position just became a whole lot more valuable.

Work relationships take a few different forms. It's important to think about how your coworkers, your bosses, and your clients affect your work, but don't forget to consider who you have access to. Learning from the top people in your field is incredibly valuable, and it's something you're likely to value. If you're an aspiring filmmaker, taking a job as a production assistant may be pretty much the least glamorous gig around. You'll probably log more than a few hours at the coffee wagon. But if you're fetching lattés and muffins for Steven Spielberg, landing that P.A. job could be an incredible opportunity.

Need another reason to value your professional relationships? Many will have the potential to become personal relationships. There's nothing like the friends we've known since childhood, but don't underestimate the budding relationships that come from day-to-day contact and shared experiences. Think about the woman sitting next to you who is dealing with the same challenges you are (and is helping you dodge your ex-boyfriend).

Or maybe you don't like to work with anyone. Perhaps you're a solitary artist who requires silence and limited professional contact. Even if this isn't your "everyday" desire, there may be periods in your career when you need some time to work unobstructed by the day-to-day contact of others.

One more thing. While it's key to think about your relationships in a strategic sense, you've also got to consider quality. Almost nothing will sap your energy and passion faster than working with people you don't trust or respect—and who don't trust or respect you. Enduring a workplace with toxic relationships is truly career suicide, and no one will care when you start to go down. But work that connects you with people you genuinely like, respect, and admire is an enormous gift. It will push you further and inspire you to give your best. No back-stabbing, nasty gossip, or mind-games involved.

PROFILE/STATUS

My best friend, Jenn, is an actor, director, and screenwriter who has built her whole career on a reputation for creativity and a commitment to her craft. Last month, she was asked to serve as a panel judge for a short film festival. The opportunity required travel and time away from her full-time job without pay. The upshot? Major profile. She hit the jackpot.

Do you value the status a successful job brings, or the profile you'll gain as you rise through the ranks? When you're building your career, profile is vital. Call it buzz, awareness, or just a good reputation, but getting your name out in the industry can give you a major advantage. If you work in a field where your efforts are highly visible—think advertising, film, television, journalism, fashion, just to name a few—profile is one of the most important assets you can have. Working undercover for the CIA? Maybe not so much.

The funny thing is, I've talked to so many young women who are afraid of profile and afraid to put themselves out there. If someone else comes knocking—a reporter who wants to interview them about a project or an award handed down from a professional organization—it's just fine. But if they have to go out there and *tell* other people about their work, they'll stop cold. Trust me on this one, building your own buzz is not egotistical or self-centered. It's smart. Just make sure you don't step out of your own style to do it. You don't have to chat up everyone you meet in the elevator and insist they peruse your portfolio. Take what comes naturally and turn it up a notch.

How important is building profile—creating a reputation others know and identify? According to the production assistant on our television series, it's not just about professional status. This twenty-three-year-old, new to the world of production, would put a hundred bucks on the fact that the sudden increase in his dating track record is all about his newfound title. How important is it for you, when asked, "What do you do for a living?" to respond with something others identify as valuable? Is that a value for you?

> I worked very hard and I earned all the attention I'm getting.
>
> —Anna Kournikova

Even if your name isn't flashing across the big screen, there are other ways to up your industry profile. Think about opportunities for networking. Time and time again, successful women say their achievements were part hard work and part great relationships that opened important doors. Could you contribute your writing to a trade journal or company newsletter? Make presentations? Take part in a client pitch, just to get face time with some of the best and brightest?

Profile also lives in the "names" connected to you and your career. Think about it. The *New York Times*. Chanel. The Guggenheim. Morgan Stanley. Leo Burnett. Harvard. The WNBA. These are companies, brands, and institutions that people instantly recognize and hold in high esteem. If you're connected to the big players, you'll immediately boost your profile. I'd never advocate working for a company or an organization on the sheer weight of its name, but if that company fits your values and your aspirations in the first place, aligning yourself with a well-known "brand" will open some incredible doors.

PASSION/FULFILLMENT

It's 8 P.M. on Sunday night. How do you feel? Excited? Fearful? Is there a nagging sense of dread creeping through your body? I've done work that elicits all these emotions as the weekend screeches to a halt, and it sure as hell feels better to look forward to Monday morning. That's not to say you won't hit tough spots. But there is nothing—and I mean nothing—better than doing work that feels right. Work that's authentic and that builds your sense of worth, rather than diminishing it.

Keep in mind that fulfillment, passion, and joy look and feel different to everyone. It's not a one-size-fits-all proposition. What can satisfying work look like?

- It makes you feel stronger, more competent, more confident.

- It gives you the opportunity to contribute something uniquely you.

- It stretches your limits.

- It gives you the chance to express yourself.

- It makes you feel valued and more valuable.

- It allows you to create change for the better.

This said, I've worked with more than a few clients whose focus has been on their personal passions in life, and what they value about their work is that they can actually leave it there. They don't have a driving, consuming passion that compels them to work into the night without time for their run, their kids, or their friends. Some of my most respected colleagues are people who have charitable passions totally and completely outside the scope of their nine-to-five job. They use work to pay the bills and to make donations to their most important causes. No judgment here. It's all about what you value.

One of the best books I've ever read about passion is *What Should I Do With My Life?* by Po Bronson. As he travels across the country interviewing dozens of people who have answered this mammoth question, Bronson weaves in his own thoughts, feelings, and revelations about finding meaning in your work. He's clear that *who you are* is inherently more important than *what you do,* but he writes about meaningful work as something that doesn't lead you to deny or fight against your true nature, but instead, actually strengthens your sense of self. Bronson writes:

Here's a refrain I heard occasionally: "All this obsession about our careers. It's not what you do that's important, it's who you are. If people stopped worrying about what they do, they'd be a lot happier. Just go get a job. Enjoy your nights and weekends."

I agree: Who you are is *more important than* what you do. The goal is to bring what you do in alignment with who you are, so you don't end up being someone you don't want to be.

I love his response, because it implies that passion can feel subtle and comfortable. It doesn't scream at you every day—or ever—and it doesn't mean that your work will be a breeze. There may still be long hours, blood, sweat, and maybe even tears. What's the key? A sense of contribution. The people Bronson interviewed work in just about every industry and profession imaginable. Many of them struggled with the idea that helping people master their golf swing, for example, can't be considered "making a contribution" when there are social workers, surgeons, nurses, teachers, and grief counselors out there doing incredible work. But Bronson provides an amazing description of what it means to contribute:

> To love what you do, and feel that it matters—how could anything be more fun?
> —Katharine Graham

> It seems that just about any profession can be performed with a confidence that it's contributing to the well-being of others—just as any profession can feel soulless and selfish. There is no official list of honorable, noble careers. The proof is in the individual's experience. You either find the pleasure of connecting with others in your daily reality or you don't—this nobility is not something that can be assigned or predetermined. Often it defies stereotypes.

Whenever you come across the word *passion*—in this book or anywhere else—think about what makes you feel most like yourself. That's passion. It lives in the moments where you're most at ease in your own skin—the moments when you feel "right," and whatever you're doing seems like an extension of your mind, body, and spirit. Whether it's scooping ice cream for a pack of hungry six-year-olds, toasting your best friend to two hundred people at her wedding, or mixing watercolors for your latest masterpiece. Passions are big or small, quiet or dynamic. Some people use their work to feed their passions, while others use their career to free themselves for other pursuits. Just how much you need to experience passion, fulfillment, and a sense of contribution *on the job* is up to you.

MONEY

Admit it: you value money. We all do. It doesn't make you greedy, it doesn't make you shallow, and it doesn't mean your greatest aspiration is to out-earn Donald Trump. The question is, how much do you value money? How important is it to you and your life?

Trust me, this is one of the most interesting, most rewarding values to understand. In my experience, it's an especially tough issue for women to get their heads around. But you need to understand your own money values, because you're making money-based decisions all the time. Every day. The more closely you match your money values with your choices, the more fully you can bring money into your life and ensure it's working for you.

> We can tell our values by looking at our checkbook stubs.
> —Gloria Steinem

There are two key questions that will help you understand your money values for the purpose of this assessment tool.

How Much Is Enough?

Be honest. Really honest. If you know you can't live with less than $5,000 a month, you've got to ensure your work will bring in more. If your weekly spa date is the difference between sanity and total breakdown, make sure you've got the cash for that seaweed scrub. We all need money. You've just got to figure out where it ranks on your list of values.

I'll say it again—be straight with yourself. In the end, a great opportunity can wind up making you feel resentful if you're not being fairly paid for your work. On the flip side, a supersize salary can start looking pretty empty if you hate how you're earning it. Money is a blank slate that we inscribe with meaning.

What Does Money Mean to You?

So, what does money mean to you? Freedom, independence, philanthropy, security, and really great shoes. Once you've covered the necessities, what do you want money to do for you or for others?

We asked these same questions in chapter One, so hopefully, you've got a good handle on your feelings about money and what you want to do with your cash—what it means beyond paying the rent or putting gas in your car. But here's the kicker. You've always got to keep these reasons in the back of your mind. They'll help you make good decisions, and make choices about money that support your true goals and ambitions. Your answer to the question, "What does money mean to me?" will be a guide as you move forward in your career and in your life.

One more thing. It's all relative. Money never exists in a vacuum. Maybe you value security, so you took that new job with a major-league salary and a hefty benefits package. But, you also value challenge (FYI: It's totally normal to have values that pull you in two different directions at the same time), and this position isn't giving your brain a creative workout. Does the money make up for the lack of challenge, or would you actually take a pay cut to flex your skills even further? It's up to you. Money is a value all its own, but it always has to be weighed against your other must-haves in order for it to really have meaning.

> Money is only a tool. It will take you wherever you wish, but it will not replace you as the driver.
>
> —Ayn Rand

YOUR PROFESSIONAL-VALUES EVALUATION

OK, now let's pull it all together. What comes next is an evaluation tool to help you examine and assess your values in totality. You might want to review the preceding value descriptions to help you assess your stance. As you go through this evaluation, remember that you're assessing the relative importance of these six values. In an ideal world, you'd have money, time, challenge, passion, relationships, and status all rolled into one perfect job. In this world, you'll probably have to put one ahead of the other. Here's how it works:

1. Rate your values—what you want to get out of your career—on a scale from one to five. One indicates that this value is not important and 5 indicates that the value is extremely important.

2. Think about your current reality, then ask yourself the questions to assess how well your values are being met. One indicates that your values are not being met at all, and 5 indicates that your values are extremely well covered.

3. Identify the gaps. If you've discovered that you value passion in your career and your heart rate barely registers a flicker as you walk through the front door, you have a problem.

Considering a new professional challenge or new job? Learn as much as you can about the realities of your new career opportunity and apply this knowledge to Step Number Two. I know this assessment can almost feel a bit too simple, but I've used this tool time and time again, and I can promise, it's surprisingly effective. If you feel like you're not getting enough out of your career but you haven't identified what more you want and need, you'll find the answers by working through this process.

In chapter Six, we're going to examine how each of these values fit in the marketplace. By evaluating your buyer's concerns and matching them

Professional Values

TIME	CHALLENGE/ LEARNING	RELATIONSHIPS	STATUS/ PROFILE	PASSION	MONEY
On a scale of 1–5, how much time are you willing to give in order to create success?	On a scale of 1–5, how important are challenge and learning to you in your work?	On a scale of 1–5, how important are your professional relationships to you in your career?	On a scale of 1–5, how important is it for you to have status/profile in your career?	On a scale of 1–5, how important is it for you to have passion for what you do in your work?	On a scale of 1–5, how important is it for you to be remunerated with money for your work?
☐	☐	☐	☐	☐	☐
1 indicates you have other priorities outside of your work that require the majority of your time. **5** indicates you are willing to work as many hours as it takes.	**1** indicates not important and **5** indicates extremely important.	**1** indicates not important and **5** indicates extremely important.	**1** indicates not important and **5** indicates extremely important.	**1** indicates not important and **5** indicates extremely important.	**1** indicates not important and **5** indicates extremely important.

Your Reality

TIME	CHALLENGE/ LEARNING	RELATIONSHIPS	STATUS/ PROFILE	PASSION	MONEY
On a scale of 1–5, does the time you're required to spend in your career seem satisfactory?	On a scale of 1–5, does your current employment satisfy your quest to learn and challenge yourself?	On a scale of 1–5, are your relationship needs being met?	On a scale of 1–5, are you satisfied with the level of status/profile your career provides to you?	On a scale of 1–5, do you feel passionate about what you do?	On a scale of 1–5, how satisfied are you with your current remuneration package?
☐	☐	☐	☐	☐	☐
Do you feel as if you have "control" over your schedule? Do you have enough time off to support the rest of your life?	Do you feel adequately stimulated? Are you encouraged to risk?	Have you built lasting relationships with people you respect? Do you have a mentor?	Do you feel respected and appreciated? Do you have the opportunity to be an influencer within your industry?	Do you wake up on Monday morning excited to start your work? Does your company have a mission? Do you believe in it?	Does your package feel fair?

with your own values, you'll be able to ensure you're relevant and ready to create the wealth you deserve. But first, chapter Five gives you some insight into what the market actually values. What is your "buyer" looking for? You'll learn how to scope out the territory, and we'll put you in the mind of that CEO on the other side of the boardroom table. Now you know what you want. Get ready to learn what *they* want.

I'm a firm believer that you can get anything you want out of your career—more money, more time, more challenge, more relationships, more passion.

You just need to have a solid sense of what you want . . . and a market that can give it to you.

wildly sophisticated icon

✳ Sarah Gray Miller
Editor-in-Chief, Budget Living *magazine*

Smart, funny, and stylish, Sarah Gray Miller heads one of the fastest-rising magazines in North America. Billing itself as the "magazine for people who want to spend smart, but live rich," *Budget Living* is a straight-talking publication that's equally luxurious, hip, and modern—much like Miller herself.

After graduating from Vassar in 1993, the Mississippi-born Miller assisted with the launches of *Garden Design* and *Saveur,* then went on to serve as the features editor for *Garden Design.* She also launched *Organic Style* magazine, which saw a 100,000-copy circulation increase in less than six months under her direction.

In 2002, Miller helped launch *Budget Living* and landed the plum job of editor-in-chief. By 2004, the magazine won a National Magazine Award for general excellence, the highest award in the industry. The same year, Miller and her team released *Home Cheap Home*—a book based on the magazine's thrifty décor ideas.

What do you value most in your work?
I just have to have a good time. I really have to be interested in it and really passionate about it. If a job is too easy and it's too much of a nine-to-five gig, I'll get bored really quickly. It's not enough to make me want to get out of bed in the morning. I have to be excited about a project, but that's not to say it's fun every minute of every day.

What excites you about your job?
It's that sense of a project. We're creating something from nothing. Also, the job offers so many different challenges. I would not want to be just a writer, sitting alone at my computer. Nor would I want to just deal with budgets and crunching numbers. Nor would I want to just edit or just deal with market research to find a great new dress. The magazine business lets you do a little bit of everything, so no two days are alike. I was here last night working with the fashion editor putting outfits together for a shoot. This morning, I was editing text. A couple days ago, I was in a business meeting talking about how to cut costs from the magazine's budget. Yesterday morning, I was on CNN doing TV. Every day there's some new challenge. It never gets boring.

What's the best investment you've ever made?
I started off making no money and working as an assistant for someone whom I really respected. There was that period of time from probably age twenty-two to age twenty-six or twenty-seven when I starved and I worked sixteen hours a day, and it wasn't easy. It really wasn't easy, but oh my God, it was so worth it. I learned everything. And instead of thinking of it as being underpaid, I thought of it as getting a free master's degree in the business.

I also had a great mentor, which makes a big difference. She worked my tail off, but she was so open and showed and explained everything she was doing all the time, and she gave me chances to fail. She was a tough boss, but she always assumed I could do things. And then, of course, my thinking was,

"Oh my God, she actually thinks I can pull this off. I don't know what I'm doing," so I would stay up three nights in a row to get it done. But I would just do it, and then she would just give me something harder and harder. I think that's the best way to learn the ropes.

How do you feel about debt?

I hate it, and I've just recently climbed out. But there is a sense of investment involved when you're young and struggling. To put it in perspective with other careers, there are lots of people who can start and be stockbrokers or investment bankers right out of college and make plenty of money, if that's what interests them. It wasn't what interested me. So, I had to struggle a bit in the short term by taking an interesting, low-paying job that in the long run has paid off beautifully, because here I am, ten or eleven years later and I am making enough money. At the same time, I'm doing something I really like to do, instead of making a lot of money when I was twenty-two and waking up at age thirty-two or thirty-three and realizing, "I'm miserable," which is what happened to a lot of my friends.

What does money mean to you?

You know, it's not important for me to have a whole lot of it or be rich. It really means a certain amount of freedom to me. And I don't mean freedom from work. It's not that. It's that feeling of being able to pay the bills and have money there. The thing that's great about having a certain amount of money—and I'm really not wealthy—but having enough to live on, is that I don't have to *think about* money. I can sit and write those checks and not think about money. If I'm lazy, I can take a cab home and not think about money. It's freedom from financial worry. I just like not having to think about it.

I just like having money so I can pay my bills and buy a cute pair of shoes. I like being able to go to the Salvation Army and buy five used coats, going to the Gap and buying a T-shirt when I want. Luxury to me is having so much underwear that I don't have to do laundry every week. This is stuff I did not have when I was twenty-three years old.

5

What Do They Want?

Understanding What the Market Values

"I'm great at giving presentations. I love getting on stage and feeling the energy of the crowd. I've completed my toastmaster's course and my evaluation was outstanding."

"That's great . . . but I'm looking for a website designer."

Do you want to create more with your career? Do you want more money, more influence, more flexibility, more control?

You need to understand the market. What's *their* more? What do *they* want?

The more you understand your market, and the better you can satisfy its needs, the more wealth you can create. In the last four chapters we've been focused on you—what you're worth and what you want. Now it's time to turn the tables. You need to thoroughly understand what the marketplace values. It doesn't matter if you're an employee or an entrepreneur, you're going to be "selling" yourself to someone. You need to step inside that someone's head and understand what she needs and what she's willing to pay for.

Think about it this way. You could be the most talented artist around. You could create avant-garde, cutting-edge masterpieces that rival the works of Picasso. But if you're attempting to sell your work to a mining company—good luck, unless they are redecorating their office. Great art is probably not their top priority. You've got to know your "market" inside out, and you've got to understand how their values line up with yours. *This is your responsibility.*

I have a client who loves creative writing. She can set a scene so authentically, you'd think you were right there. She loves to write slowly and carefully, honing every word until it's perfect. A few months ago, she submitted a few pieces to her local newspaper, and was devastated when they ripped her words apart. She came to me clearly shaken by the experience.

"I don't understand. I've always been praised for my writing, and I worked so hard on those pieces. What went wrong?"

I consulted a journalist friend for her opinion, and she gave me the straight goods.

"Nic, newspapers don't value flowery sentences or a beautifully crafted scene, without the facts and statistics to back it up—at least the news section doesn't, anyway. A newspaper values speed, efficiency, accuracy, and simplicity. That's what they have to deliver to their readers, so that's what they value in their writers."

I went back to my client and we talked the situation through. Her less-than-ideal experience didn't make her work any less valuable or satisfying to read; she just hadn't considered her marketplace. The news section was the wrong place to try her hand at publication, especially when she so honestly values artistry, time, and creative license. She set herself up for failure by focusing on her own values, without considering what her desired marketplace valued.

In this chapter, you're going to get an honest and down-to-earth view of what the market wants. These are principles that your "buyer" will rarely—if ever—come right out and explain for you. And in order to get the most from this discussion, you've got to get over yourself. Some of these ideas are scary. They require you to have initiative, to be brave, to walk your talk, and to understand how money actually influences decisions and market forces. But, these market values aren't personal. It's not about getting people to like you. With a solid appreciation of your worth and a detailed understanding of your career values, you can look your market straight in the eye and get ready to knock their socks off.

THE DOOR TO OPPORTUNITY

It's a lesson in human nature. The more we want something, the fewer questions we ask and the fewer facts we gather:

> *So what if the pipes are rusty and the roof needs replacing? Don't tell me! I love this house and I want to make an offer.*
>
> *I don't even need to read the layaway terms. This dress is perfect. I want it and I have to have it. Give me the paperwork.*
>
> *Who cares about the pay? Hire me! Hire me! I don't care whether you're ethical, interesting, or even honest. I desperately need this job.*

Trust me. I've been there too. I just finished an important capital-investment deal, and I should have asked more questions before I signed on the dotted line. This became increasingly evident as I sat down with the president of the bank for a "celebratory" lunch and finally asked him what, in his opinion, makes a great business investment. As he laid out his own personal and institutional criteria, I started to understand how I could have better positioned myself and my business. I realized that I got a good deal, but I could have bargained for a *great* deal. I also realized that his words applied equally to entrepreneurs and employees.

Are you looking to start a business? Do you need investment money? Are you trying to go after the "more" we identified in the last chapter? Are you about to switch gears or chase down something big?

The lessons I learned at the lunch were invaluable, and now I'm going to share them with you. It doesn't matter who you are or where you're at in your career. If you want someone to take a chance on you—to hire you, give you a raise, offer you an internship or fork over some investment cash—these are the principles you need to know. Grab a pen and get ready to learn from my banker.

Personal Equity

How much have you personally invested in your business or your career? One of the surest indicators of your commitment level is the degree to which you've allowed yourself to sink in. Personal equity relates to everything from the actual dollar figures you've contributed (courses, degrees, start-up cash) to the time you've invested (Have you given your career or business a good shot? Have you logged the hours you need to gain experience, understanding, confidence?). Essentially, personal equity is the degree to which you've immersed yourself in your work. Really, the more invested you are, the more likely you are to succeed. If you don't believe in yourself and your work, why should anyone else?

Beyond your personal equity, one of the first questions a financial lender will ask is, what kind of money have your friends and family invested? Even the most stoic of organizations expect those you love to pitch in before they strike a check. Their assumption is this: If you can't get people who love you to believe in your investment and, in return, to invest in you, there's a problem.

Same principle applies to employers. No, your boss-to-be probably won't ask whether Mom and Dad gave you a financial boost through college, but she does want to know that you've built on your network and you're valued by the people around you. The lone wolf makes for a great movie character, but let's face it, he probably won't be a great "team player."

Competitive Advantage

It all comes down to where you sit in the market. Who's out there doing the same thing? When I first started my business and people asked about the competition, I was like, "What do you mean? I'm doing something sooooo unique." I thought this was a great thing, but it's a little more complicated than I had expected.

Without question, you want to approach a venture from a unique perspective, but there is very likely someone, somewhere, doing something comparable and if not, there's a problem. Why? If you really do have a business that no one else has thought about, there will be the inevitable question of adequate demand. Do your research and realistically explore your competition. Competition isn't a bad thing. It's an indicator of demand; you just need to articulate how you're uniquely responding to this demand. What's your advantage—price, quality of service, unique market segment?

As an employee, you're also facing market competition. Your employer, clients, or colleagues want to know what makes you different. What makes you better? If they're facing five applicants for the same position, what gives you an edge? There are thousands of people out there who can design ad campaigns. You're not the only one who's smart, educated, creative, and driven. This is where you go back to your balance sheet. Are you ethical? Have you worked with some of the best names in the business? Have you already hit a home run in the advertising industry? If you understand your competition, you're in a far better position to play—and win— the game.

Don't Try to Hide Your Mistakes

This is related to experience. When Mr. Bank President shared this little tidbit with me, I was definitely caught off guard:

> "I want to hear about your mistakes. I want to know you've tried, floundered, and learned through the process. I'm not interested in investing in someone who hasn't experienced failure. Lack of experience, lack of failure, lack of learning is a red flag for me."

Don't be afraid to discuss your mistakes and your learning. The big shot on the other side of the desk is human and so are you. Pretending any differently is a direct route to the poorhouse.

Preparing for an interview? Let's go back to that good old standby question—"What's your greatest weakness?" Before you answer, "I'm a perfectionist," stop, I beg you. This question is a stumbling block for young women—and men—everywhere. Here's the truth. People ask about your weaknesses for two reasons. First, they want to know that you know yourself as a complete package. If you struggle with organization, for example, you're one step closer to tackling that problem. If you think you're already perfect, let's just say you'll be in for a nasty wake-up call and you probably don't have the maturity to work through challenges.

Second, the "weakness" question is all about learning—learning from your mistakes and failures. So you froze in the middle of a big presentation? Who hasn't? Public speaking is tough, and you're interviewer knows that. Hell, she may get shaky knees just hearing about your big speech. It's what you learned that counts. If you left that presentation vowing to be better prepared and more organized, signed up for Toastmaster's and then you aced your next trip to the podium, she's going to be infinitely more impressed than if you claimed to be perfect in the first place.

Sharing your mistakes, your failures, your learning, and your experience is smart. It shows you're willing to move on and to do what it takes to succeed. It shows you know yourself well. Whether you're up for a loan or a promotion, the decision-makers want to hear about your nosedives. Take a deep breath and tell the story—just make sure your tale shows that next time, there will be a happy ending.

Management/Advisers

A bank, lender, or employer isn't expecting that you know *everything* you need to know. Yes, they are looking for your leadership abilities and your expertise, but equally relevant are the people who surround you. Is your business new and you can't afford a high-caliber management team? No worries. You need to find yourself a group of "voluntary" advisers. Your advisers can come in the form of trusted professional relationships, your accountant or lawyers, for example, or clients and long-term colleagues. There are many people out there who, presented with a solid business plan, are willing to act as advisers.

In the world of work, everyone can have a team of managers and advisers—not just entrepreneurs or business owners. These people are called mentors, and they're a direct route to achieving your *more*. Not only can they open doors and offer advice, your mentors are like a good credit rating. They boost your market value by offering proof that someone else has *already* taken a chance on you. Your mentor may have a great reputation or a high-profile name that makes people sit up and take notice. Even if your mentors aren't well known, they're proof that you've taken steps to invest in your career, and that you value your work enough to ask for help and involve other people.

A word of advice in approaching advisers and mentors: Make it easy for them. I use the word *voluntary* quite loosely. Remuneration can range from equity in your business to a share of dividends, to their desire to contribute in your business vision, and to simply come along for the ride. Your mentors may just want to see you succeed. Whatever their motivations, think about how you can give back and help your advisers to see a payoff—financial or otherwise.

> The person who knows *how* will always have a job. The person who knows *why* will always be his boss.
> —Alanis Morissette

SEND ME AN ANGEL

Okay, so maybe you can't even get in for an appointment with your bank, never mind negotiating a loan. Don't give up. You need an Angel Investor—

someone who contributes to your career or your business because they believe in you. Unlike a bank or a major company, this is a relationship without any set rules. The field is open and up for discussion. Angel Investors also take bigger risks. By taking a chance on you, they may have more at stake—from money to reputations to the sheer responsibility of encouraging and overseeing your success.

As a first-time entrepreneur, many financial institutions simply won't touch you. You're an unproven commodity without the personal equity, management team, and track record the banks are looking for. This is when you start looking for an angel. From advisers to your first clients, angels come in all shapes and sizes. I consider John Duff, vice president of Penguin, as one of our first angels. He saw the full vision of our business and invested before Wildly Sophisticated was a proven commodity. Your parents might be your first angels by putting five thousand bucks in the company bank account. There are also professional, organized communities specifically looking for financial investment opportunities like yours.

If you're not a business owner, but you're trying to change industries, take on a new challenge, or find a job far different from your current position, you still may need an angel. My friend Helga is a social worker who wants to break into fashion merchandising. She's smart, talented, and inherently fashionable. She has everything she needs to succeed in her new industry—other than, well, experience, education, and contacts. She can't go to the head of Saks right now and ask for a job. She'd be setting herself up for failure. What she needs is an Angel Investor, someone who has opportunities available, and is willing to take a chance on her. Maybe it's a new designer who needs help matching her creativity with market demand. Maybe it's an independent boutique owner who needs an assistant buyer. Maybe it's a store looking for unique pieces from around the world (Helga is an insatiable traveler). She needs opportunities, not a cash injection. Her angel will offer a step forward in a new career.

What sort of angel do you need? Think widely, and don't get stuck in the traditional job/employer mind-set. Is there anyone who can offer ideas and connections that will make all the difference? If you're circumventing tradition—and let's be clear, anyone who has a career in today's marketplace is forging new territory—an angel is your key to *more*.

As we continue this discussion of angels, I'm going to divide each principle into two parts: entrepreneurs and employees—maybe you'll even fit into both categories.

The Underworld

Entrepreneur

At the height of the Internet boom, you could find an angel on every street corner. In today's market, they've become more difficult to locate. Generally speaking, groups of business people share opportunities amongst themselves. Quite truthfully, it's like penetrating the Mafia underworld, and the best way to find an angel is to get the word out on the "streets." Board of Trade meetings, business seminars put on by professional associations, your accountant or lawyer—tell anyone who will listen exactly what you're looking for.

Employee

Your network is your underworld. This is hands-down the best way to find opportunity where only doors were closing in your face. Be bold. Talk to everyone and anyone about what you're trying to do. Start with your friends and family and expand from there. Look to previous colleagues, acquaintances, even your favorite barista at Starbucks.

When Helga told me about her dream of fashion merchandising, I was shocked. Not by what she's trying to do—it's clearly a perfect fit—but because I know a woman who's opening a clothing and cosmetics boutique. It may not be exactly what Helga needs, but I'm guessing it's one step closer to a door swinging open. And remember, angels know other angels. With an "in" to the fashion world, Helga's just gained a new world of fashion contacts—all because she dared to share her big dream over coffee one morning.

The Jockey

Entrepreneur

My Angel Investor puts it this way. "I don't know a thing about career development, but I'm betting on the jockey." Prior to a million bucks in revenue, strong client relationships, and proven sustainability, all you've got is you and your passion, energy, and commitment. Most often, your angel is looking for the intangible and tangible assets we've already discussed. Do you have charisma, hope, and a willingness to work through the night? Do you have a strong set of existing relationships, your health, and some experiences with success and failure? If there is ever a time when you need to be confident in what you're doing, it's in approaching an angel—they are watching and listening very carefully.

Employee

If you've found yourself an angel, you can be sure she's betting on the jockey—she's betting on you. People will give you opportunities and chances to prove yourself because they know you've got what it takes. And if you're still looking for that angel, remember that it's all those tangible and intangible assets that will help you land one.

Helga isn't going to find work in fashion merchandising because of her background, track record, or training—she doesn't have any! She's going to break in because she's already a great jockey and she can pick up the other skills out there on the track. Her experience as a social worker means she's got patience, compassion, dedication, great communication skills, and incredible maturity. Take one look at her and you also know she's fashionable, so when the angel comes along, he's looking at her whole package. He'll be betting on Helga—not her résumé.

Equity

Entrepreneur

It's a hallmark of investment—the greater the risk, the greater the reward. If you have an angel willing to invest in you and your business at the early stages, expect to give up a big piece of your pie. There are two things you need to really think through and understand when it comes to equity. First and foremost, sit down and talk with someone neutral (not your angel) long and hard about share structure. Most angels are sophisticated investors and they know the ins and outs much better than you will.

Second, remember that angels always want something in return. They may be called "angels," but if we're talking about selfless investment, that's your Mom—not an Angel Investor. Think carefully about what you're willing to give.

Employee

No big stretch on this one. Anyone who gives you a shot wants something in return—your time, your talent, your support, or your results. Helga's going to be offering her time (probably without a lot of cash in the start), her enthusiasm, her innate talents, and her commitment—and in return, her efforts will help her angel build a stronger business or turn a higher profit.

Even if someone honestly just wants to give you a break, she still wants something back. She wants to see you succeed. She wants to see you take that opportunity and run—to make it something better than it was from the start. Never underestimate other people's desire to watch you succeed. By giving it your best shot, you're paying back your angel in spades.

READ THE SIGNALS

PricewaterhouseCoopers values money, broker blue shirts and eighty-hour work weeks. The Gotti family values loyalty, black leather, and a quick trigger finger. McDonald's values consistency, speed, and hairnets.

While we've been discussing common values in the marketplace, it's your responsibility to research and understand the nuanced values that a company (or an industry) actually *lives*. This is as true for companies as it is for people. For example, one company states that their mission is to be "the most responsible, effective, and respected developer, manufacturer, and marketer of consumer products, especially products intended for adults." They're one of the biggest cigarette manufacturers on the globe. I don't know about you, but the value of "responsibility" attached to a company that produces a deadly product is a bit hard to swallow.

Anyone can talk about what they value. But real values come through action. One of the most informative things you can do to understand the values of a company you are interested in hiring, working for, or gaining as a client, is to examine not what they *say* they value, but how they actually *act out* their values. After looking long and hard at a company's stated values, get inside and see how they live. Talk with people who have worked in the company—past clients, employees, or suppliers. And when you're considering hiring a company or a person, test them. Ask for a pitch. Do they claim to value timely, on-budget service, then deliver the proposal a week late with higher price quotes? Now you know the truth.

✳ strategy

What does your workplace value? If you're reading that corporate mission statement online, but it's still not clear what your current company or organization is all about, here are a few questions that

can help you suss it out. And here's the most important thing to remember. Values are lived, not just stated. If your company claims to value employee loyalty, but they're cutting benefits, pay, and generally making your workplace a living hell, it's pretty clear that they're more interested in money. Ask yourself:

How do my boss/coworkers/colleagues make me feel? Do I feel important? Neglected? Part of the team? Valued? Respected?

How does my organization treat its clients? Do they "talk behind their back"—i.e., claiming to value and respect a client while complaining about their requests, workload, etc.? Or do your colleagues/bosses act the same way while clients are in the room as they do in private meetings?

How often does your boss support you? Do you receive performance reviews? Constructive feedback? Learning opportunities?

What is your organization's outside track record? Is it contributing to the community? Paying employees and contractors fairly? Have there been serious internal disputes or allegations of wrongdoing? Has your company received any awards for its performance, products, or services?

Is your company innovative? Are they trying new things and open to alternative directions? Can you provide feedback and suggestions without feeling shot down? Are there opportunities for junior-level employees to interact with the "higher-ups"?

Get Inside Their Heads

While every industry and each profession will have different on-the-job values, there are a number of traits that stand out across the board. As you're moving forward with your angel, in your business or in pursuit of more, remember that you've got to stay connected to the market. Once you've found your opportunity, you've still got to keep the market happy. This isn't a one-time shot. It's ongoing. Whether you're a freelance artist, a stockbroker, a Pilates instructor, or a lawyer, your market has a few common, one-size-fits-all desires. These are the recurring "needs" you're going to face in every profession and every industry. It isn't always pretty (or politically correct), but here's an honest peek into the mind of your "buyer."

I Don't Want or Need Your Fear.

Right before Donald Trump and Mark Burnett launched *The Apprentice,* I watched an interview with these two powerful producers. The host asked Burnett, "What do you look for in an employee?" His answer, without an ounce of hesitation? "Someone who is comfortable with risk. You can't do a thing for me if you are paralyzed by fear in the face of risk."

Here's the reality. On any given day, your boss, your employer, your clients, they're scared too. As leaders, their career success has been contingent upon their ability to take risk. Risk is required for innovation and innovation is the name of the game.

Risk is a direct path to fear. If you don't feel fear, it isn't a risk. But here's the key. It's your responsibility to manage your fear for yourself. Doesn't your boss want you to be honest about your fears? Yes would be the politically correct answer; No would be the truth. The fact is, fear has this nasty way of feeding on itself. It has the potential to build into frenzied proportions and it can paralyze even the strongest of organizations. Your boss, your investors, and your clients are on the lookout for this.

Big *but* here—fearlessness has exactly the same effect. Have you ever been around someone who bravely took a risk that made you think, "Could I do that too?" Leaders are always scouting for someone, anyone, who is able to inspire them with a feeling of fearlessness. And mark my words. Fearlessness is something the marketplace values and is more than willing to pay for.

> **Fate loves the fearless.**
>
> —James Russell Lowell

I'm Not Your Babysitter.

We're talking about initiative here. Nothing has a higher value in the marketplace. I know it sounds like I'm suggesting your organization doesn't want to support you. It does, but not if you're not willing to support yourself and, more importantly, not if the cost in time and energy to support you is more than what you have to give back.

If there is anything your employer doesn't have on her hands, it's time, and in most cases, the energy to think beyond her current mountain of work. Come to the table with suggestions, solutions, and more efficient and creative ways of getting the job done and you've just found yourself a promotion.

A Merriam Webster's dictionary defines initiative as "an introductory step" and, as we all know, the first step is always the hardest. If you're the one who is willing to put yourself out there and do the things that others haven't, you've just found the key to creating abundance for yourself in the marketplace.

I Never Would Have Thought of It That Way.

If initiative is a valuable commodity in the workplace, then creativity is priceless. When the economy is tough, and even when it's not, everyone is

If you do things well, do them better. Be daring, be first, be different, be just.

—Anita Roddick

trying to do more with less. It can feel like professional Darwinism out there, and "survival of the fittest" applies to pretty much every industry around. If you can use creativity to your advantage, you just became a whole lot more valuable. A fresh perspective, a new spin on an old concept, a better mousetrap—innovation is indispensable. More importantly, people pay—and pay well—for creative work in any field.

One caveat: Make sure your creativity is well-directed and it actually improves the current situation. Developing a unique, new bookkeeping system when the existing one is lean, efficient, and easy to use will not help your office profile. The point is to make things better, not more complicated.

You Look Like Me, You Sound Like Me. You're Hired.

One of the first career books I bought was *What Color Is Your Parachute?* by Richard Bolles. He suggests that people hire employees who remind them of themselves, and he's right. I think most of us learned this one in college. Listen carefully to the professor's philosophy. Who does he quote in his lectures? What angle does he take? Who's on his reading list? And then? Repeat back in a slightly fresh format exactly what he's already told you that he believes. He thinks he's brilliant. He thinks you're brilliant. Not exactly the best way to invoke and build independent, critical thinking, but for the purposes of getting an A, it does the trick.

Yes, as I suggested in the previous section, you need to be able to think a new thought, dream a new dream, walk a new walk, but when push comes to shove, people want to hire someone who feels familiar—and who's more familiar than themselves? The public school playground, the high school lunchroom, the college sorority house—tribalism doesn't end with your entrée into the world of work.

Yeah, Yeah, Yeah, Just Get It DONE!

Have you ever been asked, "Are you a starter or a finisher?" What did you respond? Starter? So did the other 80 percent of the population. Who doesn't like the initial fun of creating new ideas, the brainstorming, the planning, the dreaming? While wrapping up those last frustrating details when the enthusiasm and fun of the project has already flatlined is not what the majority of us dream about, that is what you will be rewarded for.

> There are two kinds of people, those who do the work and those who take the credit. Try to be in the first group; there is less competition there.
>
> —Indira Gandhi

The marketplace values those who can actually get the job done. If there are one hundred talkers out there, that one person who actually takes their actions to the last and final detail (better yet, with flair and enthusiasm) will be the one who is compensated for her efforts.

MONEY AND THE MARKET

Suze Orman's *The 9 Steps to Financial Freedom* had been sitting on my bookshelf from the day it was released. I felt infinitely better knowing it was on the shelf, and I was poised to read it—as soon as I had some money to deal with.

I've shared this little secret with thousands of young women and apparently I'm not alone. The problem with this philosophy of "I'll deal with my cash once I have some" is that it's completely contradictory to the most fundamental of money laws—you're not going to get it unless you "get it."

I can't repeat this enough: I'm not a financial planner or a money expert. I never will be. What I am is a businesswoman and a career builder. I can't tell you the best way to save money, but I can tell you how to make more of it.

Initially, I was planning on using this section to highlight the textbook basics, but I've decided there are plenty of excellent places that you can find basic (and not-so-basic) financial information. Instead, I'm going to walk you through some money concepts—some common and some not so common—and build them around real-world truths.

I'd like to blame it on this crazy high school-math teacher who, back in the eighties, discovered and attempted to teach us the "new math." I was just about to get the hang of it when he threw in a backward subtraction and I was screwed. Ever since then, math is one of those skills that has eluded me. I was under the distinct impression that as long as I had a calculator I had everything I needed. I was wrong.

If you're in business—which you are, no matter if you own your own company, work for a small mom-and-pop shop, or have a desk at a multinational corporation—you need to be prepared to do the math. You don't have to be an accountant to need a level of comfort with the fundamentals of both mathematics and finances in order to create wealth. Interest rates, commissions, stock splitting—you won't always have the luxury of a calculator in the middle of a negotiation. Some basic math skills will be an infinite help. Hey, hire that kid down the street with the math book under his arm as your tutor.

Once you've mastered the basics, it's time to take a broad look at money and the market. After reading the last section, you know what your buyer, clients, bankers, or employers are looking for in your work. Now it's time to examine the money "rules" that live and breathe in the marketplace. Unfortunately, no one teaches these rules in a financial planning or business class. They have nothing to do with budgeting, spending, and saving. These hard-and-fast principles are one part sociology and one part experience. Know your stuff, learn these rules, and get ready to rake in the cash.

Low-Hanging Fruit

This is a great expression that my business partner Praveen taught me. Sometimes with the goal of proving our stuff and making our mark, we miss the easy targets.

Maybe you're out shopping for a new coat. You've picked through hundreds in pursuit of the perfect fit, color, and style. Finally, you enter one of your favorite stores and there it is: the coat that looks like it was made for you. The only problem? The price tag isn't such a great fit. You could save your cash and return to the store in a few weeks, hoping someone else hasn't nabbed *your* coat. Or, you could forget about it entirely and continue your search. There's a third option. If this is your favorite store and you're a frequent customer, how about simply asking for a discount? The store may or may not oblige, but if they're looking at a guaranteed sale—especially to a customer who will return time and time again—they may jump at it. The idea of flat out asking for a lower price seems so simple it's almost absurd. That's low-hanging fruit.

Here's another at-work example I see all the time. Young women are often eager to take on huge, pressure-laden assignments in order to prove themselves as capable and talented. They want a challenge that will propel them to stardom. Seems logical, but it's often a direct route to disaster. If the assignment gets complex and thorny and slips beyond your grasp, you're going to look less capable than before you started. Instead, try taking a routine assignment and giving it everything you've got. Add creativity, great attention to detail, and turn it into something that's really a reflection of your best ideas and efforts. The assignment's already sitting in front of you—*there's* your chance to shine.

> Love is a fruit in season at all times, and within reach of every hand.
> —Mother Teresa

Low-hanging fruit is a great concept to keep in mind, because you'll see opportunities that seemingly didn't exist before. And you'll see opportunities that others might miss. It's like stashing your best jewelry in the fridge when you go on vacation. Who would look there?

The Golden Rule

My other business partner, Paul, loves this one. We were talking with a consultant who never actually builds businesses for himself. He works for others. Let's call him Mark. One day, Mark explained that he gladly invests his time, but he doesn't invest his money. Paul responded with, "You know the Golden Rule, don't you? The one with the gold rules."

It comes down to this. The person who wields the cash—whether it's your boss, a venture capitalist, or just plain old Dad—is going to have the strongest influence over your professional life and your job responsibilities. You may or may not agree with their opinions and decisions, but if they're signing your paycheck or paying your tuition fees, you've implicitly agreed to do it their way. There are always exceptions to the Golden Rule—silent investors and parents who fund the bill without asking any questions—but in my experience, there will *always* come a time when you'll have to defer to their wishes.

Keep in mind that there are also different "levels" of gold, and money always rises to the top. If your latest pitch wows your boss, but doesn't work for your boss's boss, it's not going to fly. For that reason, you've got to know where to make requests, present ideas, and who you've got to impress. If you know your company head is looking to move product lines in a new direction, act accordingly. Even if you have to filter your projects through your midlevel boss, you'll reap the side reward of making her look good—always a great way to make the Golden Rule work in your favor.

There's one final aspect of the Golden Rule. Whether we're talking about a corporate environment, a start-up company, or a professional partnership of any sort, remember that the Golden Rule will affect how you interact with the people around you. So, like every other relationship in your life, choose your partners (and coworkers and bosses) carefully. Just like all the dates we've been on, not all are created equal. If someone's going to be "ruling," make sure you respect her values and priorities.

I like to think that for any relationship to work, whether it's personal or professional, three essential criteria must be met.

1. The Partners have to have a common goal and vision,

2. The Partners have to mutually trust the integrity of one another,

3. The Partners have to mutually trust the competence of one another.

If these three principles don't apply to your professional relationships, you're probably going to learn the Golden Rule the hard way: by doing something you really don't want to do.

Good Idea, Bad Business

This baby almost gave me a heart attack as I was first building my company. Get this: A good idea is not the same thing as a good business, or a good business decision. Anyone and everyone can love your idea, think you're brilliant, and valiantly support you, but if you can't get anyone to pay for what you're selling, you've got an idea, not a business venture. This concept is equally applicable whether you're an employee or an entrepreneur. If you want to be promoted, if you want to earn more money—figure out how to make it.

Remember the whole "New Coke" debacle several years back? Coca-Cola is probably the most iconic brand in the world. I think even pygmy tribes in Africa recognize that distinctive red and white logo and they've likely tasted what's inside. So, someone had an innovative idea. Why not build on the legend and create a New Coke? Then people would have a choice—Coca-Cola Classic or New Coke. It seemed like a great idea. Why not add another product and create an opportunity to extend the brand?

Just one problem. Turns out people love Coca-Cola because it hasn't changed. It's a classic, a standby, a reliable flavor, and a drink we all understand—whether you even drink it or not. No one wanted a *new* Coke.

Good idea, bad business decision.

Just Because You Can Doesn't Mean You Should

Most everyone will go through lean times, financially speaking. Whether you survived on rice and veggies during college or stretched your first paychecks to the limit, it takes discipline to achieve your goals with limited financial resources. It's easy to imagine all your money issues will disappear once you start earning a sizable salary, but there's a lesson in human nature involved here: The more you earn, the more you'll spend. When faced with more financial breathing room, most people loosen up their spending as well. Knowing this little truth will help you to take the money you earn (as your paychecks grow) and use it to achieve your dreams—whether that means traveling, buying a home, or building a nest egg to start your own business. The rule of thumb here is, "Just because you can, doesn't mean you should." Live within your means and make conscious, smart decisions about your money.

The chapter's introductory story is a true one. I can't even begin to tell you how many talented, skilled, charismatic, competent, "hireable" people there are out there who would get a job in a heartbeat if they actually understood something, anything, about the company they are applying to.

You're not going to sell something that your market isn't interested in buying. You're wasting your time and you're wasting their time. You have values, and now you know what the market values. It's time to put these two things together.

wildly sophisticated icon

✳ Noreen Abbasi and Sandi Hwang Adam
Cofounders, Maven Cosmetics

It's the kind of ballsy, gut-instincts story that makes you want to shake up your own career. After meeting through their extensive personal networks, Noreen and Sandi zeroed in on a shared love of cosmetics. Both had already earned M.B.A.s, worked for blue-chip financial firms, and pulled in top salaries in consulting roles, but they were ready for an entrepreneurial challenge. They quit their jobs and went to work at a makeup counter to get a firsthand look at what sells, what employees like to sell, and most importantly, what customers are looking for.

Noreen, who is of Indo-Pakistani-American and Indian descent, and Sandi, whose background is Chinese-American, could rarely find cosmetics that worked with their skin tones. So, they created Maven, a cosmetics line designed to flatter women of *all* colors and ethnicities.

The critics are raving, revenues have doubled every year, and their products are hitting counters at Marshall Field's and Sephora. It's only a matter of time before you've got a Maven product in your medicine cabinet.

✳ Sandi Hwang Adam

What's the best investment you've ever made?
This applies both financially and in more abstract terms, but I think having a wide network of contacts and building and maintaining that network is my best investment. There are people I met in my early twenties who now hold fairly powerful positions. They've taken their lives in different directions, but the network is still there. And as they've progressed, they've expanded their networks, so you find that you've got a bigger network, too, simply by keeping in touch over time. It's all about who you know, then who they know, in return.

What have you done to nurture that network?
I've just tended to naturally keep in touch with people—through the workplace and through educational experiences. When we started the business, I did start attending networking events with the sole purpose of meeting people. So, that's a more proactive step, but it's something as simple as maintaining contact over time.

What are some of the greatest misconceptions about money?
One of the greatest misconceptions is that you actually have control over your [financial] investments. I think everything you need to know about investing

is in that song "The Gambler": "You've got to know when to hold them, know when to fold them, know when to walk away, and know when to run . . . And you never count your money when you're sitting at the table." And that is completely true, because on Wall Street, investing is completely and utterly gambling.

Did you have to change any of your feelings about money or adjust your "money behavior" when you started your own business?
Well, my income went from six figures to zero, so that's pretty significant. I had to make some adjustments. My husband and I used to go out to eat a lot and we used to go out for drinks and things like that, so we started entertaining more at home. But looking back at our lifestyle when we did have money, I think we are much happier now. When I was working in consulting, our lifestyles were extremely hectic. If you ever did get a day off or a half-day off, we felt like we had to make the most of it, so we'd go to a restaurant, then a club, then to a play. We just tried to cram everything in at once and we spent money on things that were really extravagant. I feel like now that I've cut back on my extravagant spending, I've started to see what's important to me and I'm always prioritizing. It's important to me to see friends and family, so instead of going to a restaurant I might entertain at home. It's important for me to be socially responsible, so I put away a percentage of our income to give to nonprofit or charities. I actually feel more well-adjusted now that I have to sit down and prioritize.

✳ Noreen Abbasi

Have your feelings about money changed as you've gotten older?
I think women are not used to asking people for money, and as I have gotten older this has changed. I was brought up to be self-sufficient and to live within my means, so when we started the company and needed outside investment, it was really hard to ask people for that investment. But I've gotten over that for the most part. You realize it's a necessity, because if you don't have the courage to ask there won't be a company. I'm at the point where I

feel that you never know what the response might be, so you might as well just ask!

Is there something that you wish you had known when you were first starting out?
I wish I had known how much not having an income can affect you emotionally. I worked in finance, and you see very large numbers with lots of zeros at the end. You think it's just a number and you forget that it's someone's savings. You just don't make the connection—you're so distanced from it. Now, if I see $1,000, I know exactly where that $1,000 came from and what it means.

Do you feel differently when you make money now?
If I give myself an itty-bitty raise, it's the biggest deal in the world. It's more satisfying, and I'm more proud of it.

How do you deal with difficult times—both financially and in your career?
Well, you look to your friends and your family. Hopefully, you have strong enough relationships that, when you need them, they're there. And financially, it doesn't matter what's on the market if you only have a certain amount of money to spend. You learn to live within your means, and it actually forces you to be creative. And that's kind of fun. Budgeting creatively forced me to knit a blanket for my best friends baby, instead of buying her a blanket. So, it can help you to grow as well.

What does success mean to you?
I think success is when I have a set of goals or dreams and I achieve those dreams. Or at least if I haven't achieved them, then I'm on the path to achieving them. It's more about being on the path. I'm happiest that way. I'm thinking positively and when I'm thinking positively, I think that's a measure of success. When our company turns a profit, that will make it a success, but that's just one way of looking at it. It's already a success in terms of how it has affected people's lives—even in a small way. For women, it

sounds so girly, but getting a new lipstick or getting a makeover can really change your mood. Maybe not forever, but maybe just for that day or that week. And I think that boost in self-confidence is a measure of success. I also hope that our story inspires other women to pursue their dreams—that would be the greatest success yet.

Is there any advice you would give young women?

I have a huge laundry list. But I would say, if you want to start a business, you should work in the field. Sandi and I worked retail and I was a consultant to the industry, so we knew it both from the top up and from the bottom up. I think you should put together a very good business plan with projections and shop it around. Ask people to give advice on the plan and be open to criticism. Do not be afraid to ask for an investment, but put your own money in first. Invest in yourself.

6

How Do I Make This Work?

Pulling It All Together

I had a book to sell.

I knew what I valued, what I wanted from the deal, and what I had to offer. I could have sold the book, based on my own values, for about ten to twenty thousand dollars.

Nice money, but not enough, based upon the feeling in my gut of what the project was worth. I spent the next three months immersing myself in the world of literary publishing. From agency-commission structure to sales trends, I learned the business and got my head around what it values.

What came next? I pulled it together.

I value young women. The publisher values the fact that there are 20 million of these young women building careers and, most importantly, buying books.

I value career management. The publisher values the fact that this is a growing category with increasing sales trends.

I value touring the country to meet with young women who are building their careers. The publisher values the database and the contacts I've built on my tours.

I sold the book for six figures.

Creating *more* is one part knowing and being able to articulate your worth, and one part knowing and understanding your buyer's needs. The last part, and the key to creating wealth? You have to pull it together. *You* being the key word here. Defining and articulating your worth in a way that makes you valuable to your buyer is YOUR job. It's not your employer's, customer's, or investor's responsibility to figure out how you're going to make their life easier, it's yours.

Matching your values with what the market values is the killer link that most people miss. The vast majority of people are either really good at understanding their own desires or they're experts at figuring out what the market wants. If you live for either extreme, you're not going to achieve your *more* and build the success you've dreamed about.

But don't think for a second that meeting your needs *and* the market's needs is a form of "selling out" or betraying your boundaries and ethics. Let me give you an example. I have two friends, Chris and Andrea, who are polar opposites in their careers.

Chris is an illustrator with loads of natural talent. He's been drawing since grade school, and he studied graphic illustration at a local art college. He loves to bring concepts, stories, and ideas to life through art, and he's eking out a living as a freelance illustrator for a small group of independent magazines and literary journals. All would be well, but Chris wants to make more money. He values stability and he wants to be financially rewarded for his talent. Unfortunately, he isn't willing to consider the market. He thinks that anything outside what he knows—the small, low-budget magazines—means he's working for "the man." He intrinsically believes that corporate America is bad, that anyone with money is unethical, and that all commerce requires a blood-signed pact with the devil. Chris isn't willing to imagine that there are win-win opportunities out there and that, in fact, the more closely you can match your talents with the market, the more successful you'll be. He's turned down all kinds of work because it didn't conform to his rigid standards, even though it didn't cross his boundaries. Worst of all, he complains endlessly about his situation, but he's never spent the time to brainstorm and generate new options.

Andrea is a research analyst for a blue-chip financial firm in Chicago. By twenty-four, she had given up her family, a thriving relationship, and her personal freedom to log eighty-hour work weeks and to keep a travel schedule that would make a touring rock band look lazy. Andrea has spent all her time and energy spoon-feeding the market. Sure, she's been promoted and she's frequently referred to as "the chosen one" around the office, but she's miserable. She's missing out on life. And the last time I saw her, she was on the verge of a breakdown. Andrea values her relationships, her health, and her freedom, but she's stuffed those desires away to satisfy her market—her employer. And just like Chris, Andrea thinks it's all or nothing. She hasn't considered other companies or positions or even other cities to strike a better fit. She's wearing blinders, and she thinks it's selfish to put her own needs first.

Chris and Andrea are both unhappy, and they care deeply about building *more*. At the same time, they pretend not to care. They've resigned themselves to defeat without exploring their options. And trust me, the options are endless—for both of my friends. Most people think that finding happiness will require compromises, but here's the truth. The more seamlessly you can use your values to satisfy the market, the fewer compromises you'll have to make. You're creating a fit, and that fit will help you build a career that increasingly feels effortless, fulfilling, fun, and rewarding. You'll also be building more success for the people around you. You'll be doing better work, making more money, building relationships with joy and authenticity. Everyone is happy. What could be better?

In this chapter, we're going to return to the *more* you identified in chapter Four and figure out how to make it happen. Whether you want more time, passion, profile, money, relationships, or challenge—or a combination of several—the key is to determine how you can get what you want by giving the market what it wants.

This is how you pull it together.

YOU WANT MORE TIME

When it comes to time, the majority of us want more flexibility and freedom. One of the best stories I've heard about creating flexibility and opportunity in the workplace comes from the director of marketing at the Oxygen Network, Sherri Rifkin. Sherri, an incredibly creative executive and writer, had been working on a fiction manuscript for months. She came to the conclusion that, in order to really focus and complete her book, she'd need some time away from her full-time position. Sounds impossible? Sherri didn't think so. She created a game plan, a time line, and a list of reasons why her company would actually *benefit* from her sabbatical. Her bosses agreed, she got her manuscript done, and when she returned to the office, she received a promotion.

I love this story because it's both inspiring and *resourceful*. So many people believe that their employer simply would never budge, that they are too indispensable to take time away from their "work," or that it's just not possible. In 99.9 percent of these cases, this is something they've decided without thinking it through, without planning, and, most importantly, without asking.

Whether you're looking to push forward your start time to 10 A.M. so you can hit the gym every morning, or you want a three-month sabbatical to travel through Thailand, I can't imagine a more direct example of how you can make your need for flexibility relative.

As we examine how Sherri put the pieces together, you'll see what your buyer/client/boss or investor is thinking, and how you can use your values to address their needs and concerns.

Pulling It Together

"How's this going to affect me?"
This could be the best experience and opportunity for your life and even for your career, but initially, your "buyer" isn't going to see it that way. Even

if she's a master of concealing her feelings, her first response will be some variation of "How does this affect me?" The more quickly you can answer this question, the more quickly your buyer will to be able to hear, and really listen to, your request.

Be prepared for a less-than-excited response at first. Your boss or buyer may simply be surprised and need a moment to take it in. Once she has, explain what your request will mean to her. Relieve her fears. Most likely she'll be wondering if she'll have to pick up the "slack" for you, it's going to make her look bad with *her* boss or clients, or that you've got one foot out the door and this is a first step away from the organization.

"How is this going to affect the rest of the team?"

The next question from your investor, boss, or client will explore what the change in your time commitment is going to mean to your output, and to the rest of the team. Before talking with her supervisor, Sherri reviewed all outstanding deliverables, identified who could take on specific tasks, and then very wisely took her business colleague out for a drink to bring her on board. It's your responsibility to ensure your team will not be adversely affected by your time away from the office.

"Is she going to come back?"

Once they've gotten past their immediate fear or trepidation and you've clearly articulated how you're going to take responsibility to make it happen, they may have another key question: "Is she going to come back?" Sherri was smart enough to anticipate this concern. She positioned her sabbatical as something that would benefit Oxygen, and reassured her supervisors that she would be coming back. She clearly outlined her history with the company to establish loyalty and dedication, then she outlined her creative contributions over the years. She finished this portion of her pitch by explaining that the opportunity to focus on her personal creative pursuits would not take away from, but enhance, her efforts on behalf of the company—she would come back invigorated and renewed.

"Okay. Sounds good."

This might be the "thought" that surprises you most. Prior to having this discussion, Sherri had reservations. But with the support of another colleague she came to this conclusion: What's the worst that could happen? Because Sherri made her request for time in a clear, organized manner, and because she made the proposal relative and even beneficial to her employer, her request was approved just two days later. In her own words, "It was so easy. I was totally dumbfounded."

> How we spend our days is, of course, how we spend our lives.
>
> —Annie Dillard

YOU WANT A NEW CHALLENGE

A few months ago, I was interviewed by Lisa, an intern at a top fashion magazine. After we exchanged e-mails, she asked if we could chat on Sunday evening. I was happy to do it, but I couldn't help thinking "Sunday? She's going to be in the office on Sunday night?" After we ran through the questions, Lisa explained why she was burning the midnight oil. She had landed a big story for an upcoming issue, and the piece had morphed into a bigger project than anyone—including Lisa—had anticipated. She was feeling challenged in a major way and she was loving it. There were so many interviews, facts, and details still to gather, but she was determined to make it work—to prove to her bosses and colleagues that she could handle the big leagues. Lisa's need for challenge was pushing her further and higher than she'd ever been before. She was addicted to the feeling of tackling unknown territory, and confessed that she would have a hard time returning to her intern duties after this story had gone to press. More importantly, she worried that her editors would see her challenge as a one-off and she'd never get the chance to push her limits again.

Pulling It Together

"What if she screws this up and really hurts the team?"
I'm sure everyone at the magazine appreciated Lisa's initiative, but, despite her talent, drive, and dedication, her editors probably worried that she was in over her head—that her story might not be good enough for the magazine, or that she would miss important details. Your boss may love your initiative and want to find ways to keep you challenged, but not at the expense of the team and the organization. This is the piece you need to keep in mind when you are attempting to build more learning and challenge into your career. Come to a request for more challenge with a plan. Be prepared to explicitly describe how you will tackle the challenge. Explain how you will access support if you need it. Indicate the "milestones" or "triggers" you are going to be looking for to indicate you need to take the challenge in a different direction, then get ready to explain your contingency plan.

"I'm impressed."
For the most part, challenge and learning are always up for grabs. Lisa wanted the story so badly, and she knew she had the right background to pull it off, so she asked her boss to give her a shot. Clients, investors, and employers expect you to take initiative. They expect that you are committed to learning, and they want to support you in challenging yourself. I can promise that, even if your "buyer" feels as if the challenge is too risky, you will gain respect for your desire to try.

"There's just too much at stake."
If you sense your buyer isn't biting the challenge bait, it's likely because there's too much at stake. Be straightforward; ask the question, What are you afraid of? If you're in a situation like Lisa's, where you're an unproven commodity, ask for a smaller, less "dangerous" challenge in order to prove your money is where your mouth is.

I'm happy to report that Lisa's story was a hit. She wrote the piece with

All adventures, especially into new territory, are scary.

—Sally Ride

creativity, clarity, and, to her editor's delight, bulletproof accuracy. She came out of her challenge unscathed and with a newfound sense of respect in the office. I'm sure her internship is soon to become something much more permanent and well-paid. Not only that, she's ensured her work will always involve challenge and learning. That's the thing about challenge. Polish off what's on your plate, and the dessert cart is inevitably around the corner.

YOU WANT TO BUILD NEW PROFESSIONAL RELATIONSHIPS

Uncertain of what I wanted to do next in my career, I spent some time considering going back to school for another degree. My grandmother had been planning a trip to London, England, and with Cambridge on my list of potential schools, I decided to tag along. My first call prior to departure? The dean of admissions.

A big part of getting more is accessing those who can actually give it to you. I'll admit it. The thought of cold-calling the dean gave me shivers. But the thought of passing up the opportunity to meet with him scared me even more. I swallowed my fear, picked up the phone—and in minutes, I had an interview scheduled. Relationships are essential for career and business success, and there are three things to remember in the face of a shaky dial hand:

- Most people assume that the higher someone is on the ladder of success, the more difficult they are to access. They're wrong. In fact, because the majority of people would never think to ask, these people are often the most likely to grant you their time.

- Who doesn't love to be identified as an influencer in their industry? If there's one thing you can always count on in getting access to the big and powerful, it's some level of ego. An authentic compliment, a passionate request, and a bit of humility are usually all it takes.

- Just as you can count on ego, you can equally count on a commitment to help. Mentorship is the key word here. People really do want to help you. They just need to believe they have what you're looking for, that you are going to be taking responsibility for actually *doing* the work, and that it's not going to take more time or energy than they actually have to give.

- I'd almost guarantee there are people surrounding you and your life whom you need to get to know. As we work to create profitable relationships, we often miss the people who are sitting right there in front of us. Start talking about what you're after.

- Remember that there are always "little people" attached to every big name and every high-profile mogul out there. And I use the term *little people* with the utmost dose of irony. These are the people who *truly* hold the power. That secretary, personal assistant, or production coordinator is also a gatekeeper, adviser, therapist, and more-valuable-than-a-million-bucks lifeline to the bigshot you're trying to access. Just ask my beloved office manager, Rox. If anyone gave her trouble, I'd be on their ass faster than you could say "the deal is off."

Pulling It Together

"If I answer this e-mail or return this call,
will she call me every single day?"
Be clear that you're not a stalker. Choose your words carefully. You are attempting to build a reciprocal relationship here. You want to be respectful and nonthreatening. Don't say, *"I need you to respond. I will keep calling until I hear from you."* Think about how eager you'd be to talk with this person.

*"I haven't even called my sister in a month.
I don't have the time to maintain this relationship."*

This is just like courting a new potential beau—calling him three times a day, *every day,* is not the solution. We're all busy and while, yes, there is power in persistence, you need to be very clear that you respect your contact's time, understand the basic nuances of relationship-building, and you're not expecting her to become your new best friend.

"I don't even know that I'm going to be able to help her with what she needs. I might be wasting her time."

As I suggested in the second point in the list above, you absolutely want to start your communication with a focus on your contact. Take the time to learn a bit about her, and ask if this is a good time to chat. But what you don't want to do is leave your contact wondering what in the world you need or want from her. If the call is simply to authentically compliment her—let her know. If it's to ask if she'd meet for an informational interview, get to the point. Ambiguity breeds fear, and if your contact is afraid of you, she won't be calling you back.

> **If the career you have chosen has some unexpected inconveniences, console yourself by reflecting that no career is without them.**
>
> —Jane Fonda

"Now she wants something from me."

It's not the time to befriend that woman in Accounting when you need a rush on your expense check. You want to be building relationships at all times with everyone. Respect people for what they do, regardless of what you need in return.

In the end, I chose not to go to Cambridge. I realized that I just wasn't up for another classroom—the exams, papers, tuition fees, greasy campus food, and all. But, I've kept in touch with the dean of admissions to this day. No, he's not exactly at the top of my Christmas card list, but we exchange e-mails now and then, and when something big happens in my career, I let him know about it, and he keeps me up on what's new at Cambridge.

Who knows, maybe one day I'll be itching for that M.B.A., and, if and when that happens, I've got a solid relationship to pave my way. You never know when a strong contact or friendship will make all the difference.

YOU WANT MORE STATUS OR A HIGHER PROFILE

Status, profile, respect—whatever you call it—this is all about being "known" in your industry. And who doesn't want to be known as talented and valuable? While profile is something you build on your own, other people play a hand in how public your work becomes, or how many doors open to you. Common sense would assume that building profile doesn't take much cooperation from the person on the other side of the desk, but think again. If we're talking about status, we're getting into a really tangled web of human nature and mixed emotions. Even when your employer, client, or investor has the best of intentions, they may feel conflicted about your push for profile.

Pulling It Together

"Will you get too big for your britches?"

I first heard the term *host disease* when we began filming the pilot of our television series. At first, I thought, "What are you talking about?" Then I started to hear stories from across the industry. It seems the spotlight has a strange way of either bringing out the best in people—think Oprah—or highlighting the worst. Just because you're in front of the camera (or at the head of the boardroom table or captain of the rowing team), you've got to keep the public aspect of your work from going to your head. Help the people around you to understand *why* you want more profile, and calm their "big head" fears.

"Will we lose her?"

When you're valuable to a business or a client, people want to hang on to you. They may worry that boosting your profile might send you right into a new stratosphere—one that makes you too expensive or too in-demand to stick around for them. It's the head-hunting phenomenon in action. If people know you're here to stay, they'll be much more likely to help you achieve greater profile.

"Will your glow diminish mine?"

This is the uglier, human-nature side I was talking about earlier. But it doesn't have to be bad. It's easy to think that when someone else gains profile, you inevitably drop a notch. Nothing could be further from the truth. Excellence breeds excellence, and achievement is unlimited. Just because someone else is successful doesn't mean that your chances are suddenly diminished. If you're negotiating for more profile, respect, or status, it's important to focus on how your achievement will enhance your "buyer's" profile in the process. Think about it. A star employee, one who's quoted in the media and respected in the industry, only makes the company look better, and boosts the organization's public image. Focus on the win-win situation.

> Some people obtain fame, others deserve it.
>
> —Doris Lessing

YOU WANT MORE MONEY

I've saved the best for last. My guess is that you picked up this book about money and investment because you're looking to make more. The key to making money relative is to understand what people pay for. Let's put the ball in your court . . .

Imagine you're walking down Madison Avenue in New York City. You peek inside a window and see a Kate Spade bag that inspires a huge wave of desire. You're suddenly rationalizing why you absolutely need it, bargaining with yourself to take the subway rather than a cab for a year, and wracking your brain trying to figure out how to extend that line of credit.

One of the most effective ways to understand the basic relativity of value is to watch yourself as a consumer. As you walk up to the cash register, ask yourself what emotions triggered your purchase. What do we pay for? Here are a few of the basics:

Something we simply can't provide for ourselves
Stitching up that Kate Spade bag.

Something we would rather not do ourselves
Think manicure.

Something that makes life easier
I'll have an order of Pad Thai to go.

Something that makes you look better in the eyes of others
The unread copy of *Crime and Punishment* you keep on your bookshelf.

Something that makes you feel better about yourself
You gym membership (even if you don't use it).

Last, but not least: We pay for what's rare and less attainable
When Madonna's having trouble scoring the latest Louis Vuitton clutch, you know that baby's going to be priced through the roof. It's the law of supply and demand.

Pulling It Together

"What am I going to get out of it?"
This is the critical and central question for the banker, investor, or employer sitting on the other side of the desk and you'd better be ready to spill. Of all the values we've discussed, money is the one thing the large majority of people

Money can't buy happiness, but it can make you awfully comfortable while you're being miserable.

—Clare Booth Luce

will not give more of without knowing specifically what they are going to get back in return. The listing above indicates what people will give up their cash for, but in many instances, it all comes down to a trade for a trade.

This is incredibly simplistic but let's run down the list. Your banker wants money in the form of interest. Your investor is looking for dividends and/or equity. Your employer wants to make money from your efforts. In essence, the best way to negotiate for more money is to clearly illustrate how you're going to earn more for someone else. Before you approach anyone for more money, you have to clearly understand what and how they are going to get back—and the bigger the better.

"What if I get hurt because of this?"

Two words here: credit risk. Your banker, your employer, your investor, your vendor—beyond understanding what they will gain, they need to know they will not get *hurt*. Any investment involves risk, but one of the best ways you can mitigate this risk in the minds of your buyers, is to prove that you are trustworthy, that you are disciplined, and that you can create results *before* you ask for one red cent. So many young women fail to build their money relationships before they actually need money. We talked about this earlier in the book, but it's worth repeating: Your first visit to your bank manager should not be when you're strolling in to ask for a loan.

"I simply can't afford it."

I'm a big believer that if the exchange is right, your buyer will find the money, but here's a big lesson I learned right after graduating from university. Wanting to buffer my account with some extra cash, I kept the part-time hostessing job I had during college after I landed my first real career position. I kept at it for months, until I told a few professional peers (not my boss!) what I was up to on Friday nights. Within days word got out, and I was introduced to someone looking for a researcher on a book she was writing. I went from twelve bucks an hour to one hundred and fifty. My talents didn't change, my effort level didn't change—my marketplace changed. There's something important to learn from knocking your head against the wall, asking for more from the wrong source. If you want to make two hundred thousand dollars as an accountant, go to Ernst & Young, not a tiny nonprofit organization.

"I can't afford NOT to give it to her."

Some skill sets are remunerated more than others. Why is Sarah taking your order at McDonald's for minimum wage? Because there are literally millions of people who can do that job. Why does Meg Whitman, CEO of Ebay, command top dollars? It's because she's doing something most people cannot do.

It's the whole "We pay for what is rare" concept from above. If you know *they can't afford not to* give you what you want, you've just stepped closer to success. I can't even begin to tell you how often I see women underestimate their contributions. You are valuable. And your goal is to ensure you are increasingly more so each and every day. Spend some time working through the following questions. What are your salable talents and skill sets? Which of these are unique? How can you continue to develop them into a specialty that others will pay for?

"Can I take this person for a ride?"

Are you waiting for money to come your way? Waiting for your credit card company to suggest a lower interest rate? Waiting for your boss to ask if you'd like a raise? Don't hold your breath.

I believe people are good, but greed and money are the two things I've seen that can really turn people bad. You need to protect yourself against the possibilities. You need to understand and take responsibility not only for understanding what you're worth in the marketplace, but how money affects the market—and the people who are part of it.

It's true. I sold the book for six figures by ensuring that my values (young women, career development) worked to their best

advantage in the marketplace (book sales, profile, and an ongoing partnership with my publisher).

But here's the funny thing. My "sale" didn't end after we signed that contract. I'm constantly managing this relationship and working to stay relevant in the market—to make life easier for my publisher, editors, and agent.

It's like an equation that you've got to keep running. Do the numbers add up? Are your values still well aligned? Is the relationship mutually beneficial? Pulling it together is never a one-time deal. To achieve your more, it's something you've got to do on an ongoing basis.

In the next chapter, we're going to take a hard-and-fast look at sales. Once you've pulled it together, it's time to close the deal. Get ready for the good stuff. This is where your vision becomes reality.

wildly sophisticated icon

✳ Sally Hogshead

Creative director and advertising mastermind

Armed with humor, charm, and one of the sharpest minds you'll ever meet, Sally is like a hurricane force in the advertising industry. She began her career at Wieden & Kennedy and Fallon McElligott, working as a copywriter for high-profile accounts such as Coca-Cola, Nikon, and BMW. In her second year of advertising she won more awards than any other writer in the country, an unprecedented six One Show medals. At age 27, she opened her own agency, Robaire & Hogshead, which quickly won awards from every major show in the industry. In 2001, Sally founded the West Coast office of the number-one agency in the country, Crispin Porter + Bogusky, working on accounts like MINI and Ikea. Today she consults around the country as a writer and creative guru. A mother of two, Sally calls herself the "under-achiever" in the family—her sister won three Olympic gold medals, and her brother graduated from Harvard.

What does money mean to you?
Fabulous new shoes! Okay, seriously, I admit, I have a love/hate relationship with money. I think most women do. We make it "mean" something personal. My girlfriends will talk about all kinds of private stuff—bikini waxes, marital problems, you name it—but we'd never dream of comparing salaries. A paycheck can feel too much like a scorecard. Guys aren't as uncomfortable with that kind of competition, but it makes most women squirm. Besides, my husband is a stay-at-home dad, and his "job" of raising our kids is infinitely more important than mine. My job just happens to come with a check attached. The money itself is only a means to an end, not a value judgment of our contribution.

Did you always know what you wanted to be in advertising?
As soon as I started creating ads, I fell head over heels for the whole creative process. I've always been kind of a dork about work because I really, really love my job. Being paid is only a by-product. What's depressing is meeting someone who's miserable in a crappy job but can't leave because she doesn't have the skills, experience, network, or reputation to exit. That kind of situation is tough to turn around, but it can be done, and it should be done as quickly as possible. You can't reach your ultimate potential if you don't genuinely adore what you do.

What's the best investment you've ever made?
Investing in myself. No question. When I first started out, I made a conscious decision that I'd put my whole heart into to producing the best work I could, and gain the most valuable skills and experience, even if it meant eating Ramen noodles every night. I moved across the country five times to work at the top agencies, always focusing on long-term goals over short-term bottom line. A few years ago I quit an extremely well paying job to take one that paid

50 percent less because it gave me the chance to work alongside insanely smart people. And yes, it absolutely paid off.

How has that investment paid off?

That early focus jump-started my career. But more importantly, it created more options for my work, my family, and our future. It allows me to control my career, rather than being controlled by it. My husband and I get to decide how, where, and when I'll work. How cool is that? Top employees always have power, because they can walk away. So by investing in yourself, you earn something infinitely more powerful than money: you earn the power to choose your life. Well worth the Ramen noodles.

What do you look for when you're hiring?

I look for visionaries. Someone can learn skills for becoming great, but they can't learn vision. You've either got it or you don't. And I've always found that the best visionaries are a little crazy. They're rebels. They refuse to be constrained by the status quo. When I find someone like that, I'm incredibly excited. They're the ones who can light the world on fire.

7

How Do I Sell Myself?

Asking for What Your Worth

Me: *OK, so what's your bottom line?*

Photocopy Salesman: *I was hoping you would tell me.*

Here's the joke of all jokes. You can think about what you're worth, decide on your values, explore the market values, put it all together and still be left with *nothing*. You are never going to get what you don't ask for. More often than not, the willingness to actually put their "price" out into the ring is what differentiates those who are actually getting *more* from those who are just thinking about it.

What makes us so afraid to actually make the sale? My guess is that our stereotypical images of a sleazy used-car salesman, or telemarketers who have the uncanny ability to disrupt a rare dinner at home are partly to blame. The other, more important part?

We simply don't know how.

If you're going to build more—more success, more money, more freedom—you've got to not only come to grips with the concept of sales, you need to learn how to close the deal. It comes down to this. In the world of work, we're all selling something—whether it's real estate, our skills and talents, or our ideas, creativity, and determination—and the key to selling is not only deciding what you *have* to sell, but what you're *willing* to sell. The sales process is based upon truth, authenticity, and a strong degree of understanding about yourself and your buyer. You've got a lot more than your looks, your car, or your killer wardrobe to sell, but it's all part of the package.

In this chapter, we'll cover the finer points of selling. You'll learn all about the power of leverage in the sales process, and use the Wildly Sophisticated "sales commandments" to boost your confidence and achieve the results you're after. We'll talk about authenticity, and how the best sales come from a place of truth, fairness, and equal opportunity.

> **Pennies do not come from heaven. They have to be earned here on earth.**
>
> —Margaret Thatcher

Finally, we'll get down to the nitty-gritty details of negotiation. Whether you're vying for a new position or buying a car, this step-by-step guide will help you see negotiation in a new light. The last step? You've got to make it personal. Sales is all about relationships, and forging a solid connection is the best way to ensure your "buyer" keeps coming back for more.

Get ready to hit the market and seal the deal. This is an exciting part of the process—it's truly the point where your dreams become a tangible, touchable reality. Learn to sell with confidence and nothing and no one can stop you.

WHAT CAN YOU LEVERAGE?

Right after the first season of *The Apprentice* hit the airwaves there was one hot topic at watercoolers nationwide. It's not the first time we've heard this question, and it won't be the last. But everyone suddenly wanted to know, "Is sex appeal an unfair advantage for women in the workplace? Is using sex appeal right or wrong?"

Leverage is all about gaining a "positional advantage" to give you added clout, power, or influence in a sales transaction, a relationship, or a career negotiation. Sex appeal isn't the only advantage you wield—and leverage isn't a concept that's only useful at work. When you've made dinner three nights in a row and your boyfriend balks at doing the grocery shopping, you've got a positional advantage on your side. Your culinary track record puts you in the more powerful stance to negotiate—and win—the grocery-shopping struggle.

Anytime you go into a "sales" situation, think about what you've got to leverage. What's your positional advantage? What can you use to raise the stakes just a little higher?

Let's say you want to work from your apartment two days of the week. You've got your home office all set up, and, more importantly, you've got the discipline to actually get out of bed in the morning and resist that three-hour "lunch and soap opera" break. Think about what will help you to convince your boss that it's a good idea. Do you have a long commute to the office? Do you need a quiet environment to really focus and get down to work? Those are the basics. Now, consider your positional advantage. Have you already proven that you work well away from the office—on a business trip, for example? Are you known for your competence and dedication? Can you offer a trial period and write an end-of-the week report that outlines what you've accomplished?

It's like going to court (or watching *Law and Order*). Make a list of what you've got to back up your case, then provide tangible evidence to support your argument. That's leverage. Now, enjoy your work-at-home days— bunny slippers and all.

Here are some of the strongest advantages you may have to leverage.

Balls

It's one thing to dream big and make plans. It's quite another to jump in and actually do what scares you. When people can count on you to make the hard phone calls, have the uncomfortable conversations, and overcome the rough spots on the road, you've got a major advantage.

Knowledge

Your customer needs something. You've got great ideas and the problem-solving skills to work your way out of even the stickiest challenges. If you've got the answers, you're going to be a giant step closer to sealing the deal.

Momentum

I learned early in my career that people love momentum. They love to see accomplishment, and the energy that builds when ideas are put in action. So, here's how it works. Whenever I get a piece of good news, or something significant happens in my business, I make sure my investors know all about it. A quick e-mail, and I've gained a little more leverage. It's not a gimmick—it's a way of demonstrating that you follow through on your plans, and that you've got the ability to make big things happen—quickly.

Competition

It's the headhunter phenomenon. When someone else is interested in you and your work—you've got another job offer, someone else wants that prize painting, you can't take on the account because you're fully booked—you gain a powerful form of leverage. Competition makes you look popular and in demand. And as you've probably experienced with an ex-boyfriend or that gorgeous (but very married) trainer at the gym, most things become more attractive when you know you can't have them.

Sex Appeal

So, let's get down to the interesting stuff. Sex appeal—advantage or disadvantage? We'll take some extra time on this one because there's very little out there to help guide your way. Quite frankly, this topic is complicated and very, very personal.

Here's what I know. Sex appeal is a powerful tool, and just like operating any powerful instrument, you need to know how to handle it. You also need to be prepared for the responsibility that comes with using that tool.

> Quirky is sexy, like scars or chipped teeth. I also like tattoos—they're rebellious.
>
> —Jennifer Aniston

It's not one or the other.

Sexy and smart are not mutually exclusive. It comes down to the story I told in *Wildly Sophisticated* about being caught with *The Beauty Myth* in one hand and the latest issue of *Cosmo* in the other. One of the things I find most disturbing about the whole sex appeal debate is the assumption that women with sex appeal lack intelligence and ability. You can be, and in fact need to be, *both*. Please know that "sexy" without sustainable intelligence, focus, and performance will not create career success.

It's not about being a textbook beauty.

Sex appeal is not about looking like Naomi Campbell. I have seen many untraditionally attractive women use sex appeal like nobody's business. What is sexy? While for the most part, just like beauty, it's in the eye of the beholder, there are a few characteristics we're all generally attracted to, in men and in women. Intelligence, confidence, charisma, the ability to command a room, mysteriousness, just to name a few. Sex appeal is about attitude, not looks.

Sex appeal is not the same as sex.

Let's be crystal clear here. Sex appeal is NOT the same as sex. I'm not talking about leveraging your body to create money or success. That has a different name: *prostitution*. Using sex to get what you want in the world of work is one of the most dangerous and ineffective strategies I know. Please be fully aware that if you actively use this strategy, you risk a couple different things. One, word will get around and you will lose credibility, respect, and influence. Two, don't kid yourself. There are double standards around women and sex. If you have sex for financial or career leverage, know that if the relationship sours, you will be the one walking out the door, not him.

It's a two-way street.

I had two meetings one Friday, one with Saks Fifth Avenue and the other with Dress for Success—the fabulous organization that gives business suits and a boost of confidence to women in need. Each meeting required a different level of energy, a different approach, and because I had the time, a different outfit. The art of sex appeal has everything to do with the person sitting on the other side of the table. It's not just about what makes you comfortable. I can promise if the person on the other side of the desk is disturbed by your attempt to leverage your sex appeal, it's a definite disadvantage.

There's a line.

And once you pass it, it's difficult to come back. The challenging thing is that the "line" is so difficult to define. You might find examples in your personal life more prevalent than in your professional one, but I'm guessing you've seen it—and it isn't pretty. It's all about you, the other party, and the energy you have between you.

MAKING THE SALE

Everyone's got a customer. It doesn't matter if you're a singer, a banker, a copywriter, or the head of a nonprofit organization. In the first few chapters, you figured out what you're after, and you learned how to match your goals with the needs of the market. Now you're ready to sell.

Leave all those images of the tire-kicking salesperson and your fear of appearing pushy and indulgent at the door. In the world of work, selling is the link between ideas and results. It means someone will actually read your screenplay or hang your paintings in their gallery. It means your boss gives you that high-profile project you've been after. It means you've got the venture capital you need to get your business off the ground. Selling takes you from the abstract to the tangible—an amazing place to be.

So, here's the best news. Everyone's heard the cliché phrase "He's a born salesman," but you can actually learn how to effectively sell your ideas, your products, and ultimately, yourself. And once you get more comfortable with the pitching and selling process, the closer you'll be to success. Here are my Wildly Sophisticated sales commandments.

You've Gotta Believe

If there's any message you take away from this section, I hope it's this: You can't sell it if you don't believe in it. This is where you differentiate yourself from the sleazy electronics salesman—and I don't care what you're pitching. Maybe you're selling water to some of the biggest hotel chains in the world. How much do you really care about water? Well, if you know you're selling the cleanest, freshest water around, and it's going to keep people healthy and safe, you'll feel a whole lot more enthusiastic about the process (and the product).

And here's the truth: People know when you're lying. They can sense authenticity in their gut. They can sense whether or not you really believe in what you're selling. If you know your photographs are among the best on the market, that belief will come through in your sales process, you can't help it. Your eyes will light up, your expression will lift, your hands will begin to talk for themselves. If you truly believe you're right for the job, and you know why it's such a great fit, selling becomes natural. It's easy, and it doesn't feel uncomfortable. If you're uncomfortable about what you're selling (and in an interview process this may mean you)—if it feels wrong, or you know the claims and promises are overblown—it's time to step back and reevaluate what you're doing. Think miracle diets or instant hair removal. Not only are you setting yourself up to fail, selling something that clashes with your values is the quickest way to undermine your confidence and self-esteem.

Sell It Soft

I learned this baby the hard way. New to the sales process and in the middle of my first million-dollar deal, I slammed down my fist on the boardroom table and said as emphatically as I could, "This is the best product on the market." Impressive? Not so much.

The CEO of the company pulled me aside the next day and taught me a little lesson about the soft sell. "You need to walk the buyer into making the decision you want them to make, and you don't do that by jamming it down their throats. You need to lead them to believe this is the most logical choice they could make."

We've all heard the hard sell. "No payments until 2008! No interest! No money down! Flat abs while you sleep!" But after the five hundredth hard sell, you just don't care any more. In fact, the only way you could care less would be if you heard the pitch a few more times. The soft sell is much more subtle. It assumes the person on the other side of the table is smart, savvy, and would logically come to the same conclusion—you deserve the raise.

There are times when you're going to push it a little further, and when your sell will need to be straightforward and direct. The key is to ensure you never cross the line between passion and desperation. How do you know when you've gone one step too far? In my experience, your body makes it pretty clear. Heart thumping, palms sweating, you're actually getting more nervous and losing focus as the process continues. Your body is screaming, "Stop!" but you just keep going. You've crossed the line, and your buyer will feel it too.

Maybe you're approaching your boss to ask for a raise. The key mistake so many young women make here is focusing on the asking, rather than the selling. You don't want to harass or corner her, or make your boss feel pressured and uncomfortable. You'll get so much further if you walk her through your own thinking process:

"Since I've taken on those two client accounts, I believe my work has become much stronger and more valuable to the company. I've personally increased ad sales by five percent, I've attracted three new clients and I've worked with every different department to maximize this campaign. Given my new responsibilities and my contributions to the company, I feel my work should be remunerated with a higher salary."

It's a soft sale—firm, but soft. Your boss will still feel that you've given her a choice. Your request is respectful, but detailed, and the pitch is solid.

Read the Room

You're polished and practiced. You strut into your buyer's office ready to conquer the world. One problem. She's distracted, stressed, and more than a little grumpy. It may be worth asking if there's a better time to meet. She just may be relieved that someone—anyone—noticed what's going on and has some empathy for the situation. If she's determined to continue, keep watching for clues. This may not be the time to push. Leave her with some supporting information, and schedule another meeting.

Even if you've got a calm, relaxed person (or group) at the other end of your pitch, it's always important to read the room. Watch for clues, and adjust your presentation accordingly. You don't have to be a mind reader, just feel the energy. Are people excited? Interested? Watch their eyes, and gauge how they react to different parts of the pitch. Emphasize the ideas that make them sit up a little straighter and lean in close. You'll know you're making headway when the buyers begin to engage. That means they're asking detailed questions and putting their own scenarios on the table: "So, if we were going to carry your handbags here in Saks . . ." They may give counteroffers, or ask for different terms.

Know What's on the Line

Okay, back to selling water within the hotel chain (there are people who actually do this). You'll improve your results, and ensure a beneficial deal, if you can figure out how to make it relevant to the person on the other side of the desk. In this case, I'm not just talking about the hotel chain. I'm talking about the woman who's in charge of new products and vendor agreements. What is she trying to accomplish in her work—and her career? Does she need to look like she's on the cutting edge, or is her job to build great partnerships? Who is her customer?

Just as you've got goals and a larger purpose behind your "sale," so does the person you're selling to. This may take a little digging, but figure out what she wants and needs—personally—and you've just entered a whole new level of sales. Now it's about a mutually beneficial outcome, for you, for her, and for the entire company. What's better than that?

Find an Advocate

If at all possible, you want to be pitching to the decision-maker, but chances are your first pitch won't go straight to the top. You won't be asking your company CEO for that new client account. You'll be asking your boss. Your financing plan won't go to the president of the bank, but to a branch manager or a loan specialist. Think of these people as your advocates. You've got to knock their socks off, no question, but the sale may not end there. Your boss may have to repitch your idea to her boss, or to the CEO. She's now got a sale of her own. In this case, give her the tools she needs to make it happen.

When I was creating Wildly Sophisticated, I developed a few key phrases and ideas that clearly explained what I was doing:

We're redefining career development.

We're making it fresh, edgy, and sexy.

Young women see their lives through the lens of their careers.

Work is where they challenge themselves, reach for more, meet their friends—and even where they date.

I've got to admit, there were times when I felt like a wind-up doll after telling the same story for the hundredth time. Still, I had to remember that people were coming fresh to the concepts I had been hammering out for years. It was my job to give them the tools—the words, phrases, key ideas—that would help them make a great sale, and achieve their own goals. You can do the same.

Make It Fun

I had been searching high and low for the perfect dress. I could see it in my mind's eye, for a very special event. I wanted to look fantastic, poised, sophisticated—I wanted to make an impact. As a last resort, I pulled into a boutique store filled with dresses that would require a second mortgage to actually purchase. Jenn and I looked around tentatively, fingering the dresses longingly, when a saleswoman approached and said without an ounce of hesitation, "I have the perfect dress for you." I turned to face her with the "Yeah, yeah, whatever" look in my eyes. "No, I really do," she said. I described what I needed, and she looked conspiratorially at Jenn and asked if she'd mind taking me to the dressing room.

The next three hours were the some of the most fun of my whole shopping life! The dress was, in fact, perfect. She then came with a glass of champagne, the

> One out of forty American men wears women's clothing. We've had more than forty presidents. One of these guys has been dancing around the Oval Office in a prom dress.
>
> —Allison Janney

perfect shoes, a wrap, and a piece of lingerie that would be tailored (at no cost) to fit the dress perfectly. Trying on beautiful clothes is always a delightfully fun process, but Karen, my new friend and saleswoman, made the experience an *event*.

I bought the dress.

When we're looking to "buy" something, we naturally consider need, price, and fit (for our body and our lives), but there's another, more subtle element. From clothes to consulting to employees, we also "buy" the best experience. When you make the sales process fun, not only will you relax and let your personality come shining through, but your buyer will feel infinitely more interested and invested. Selling can be tough, but it shouldn't be painful. Make it fun and you'll be a giant leap closer to making the deal of your dreams.

Sell Big

The concept of selling big is exceedingly obvious, but often overlooked. It's also the one thing that has affected my success more than anything else. When I was first starting out, all those with an opinion told me to start small—to sell my book to a local publisher; rather than a television series, everyone suggested I create a documentary and start from there; forget *Elle* magazine, try to get a piece in the local paper. I had already read *Jitterbug Perfume* and had a taste of Tom Robbins's quote: "To achieve the marvelous it is precisely the unthinkable that must be thought." I was ready to sell big.

Keep in mind that there's a clear line between selling big and the "hard sell" we discussed earlier. Selling big means you're pitching to the strongest, most rewarding market you can reach. It doesn't mean that you're going to be pushy, forceful, and demanding. All the same sales principles apply equally, if not more essentially, when you take your pitch to the top. Overwhelmed? There are two key things I've learned that will help dilute your fear of the big sell.

Bigwigs don't (usually) bite.

I was sitting in a restaurant waiting to pitch the editor-in-chief of *Elle* magazine. As she walked through the door, she looked exactly as I expected: Hèrmes scarf loosely, but expertly, tied around her neck, perfectly applied makeup and coiffed hair, the posture of a post. What I wasn't expecting was how down-to-earth, unpretentious, and downright kind she was. One of the things that can stop us from selling big is the perception that our buyer is larger than life. The truth of it is, we're all human. CEO, editor-in-chief, president, executive producer—behind these titles are real-life people who have quite likely been in your shoes. They're not nearly as scary as you'd think.

It's worth the effort.

"It takes so much more work to sell big." If you're working from the Wildly Sophisticated perspective of excellence, you're already putting your best effort into the process, regardless of who's on the other side of the table. Once you've committed your very best effort, get this: It's going to take the same amount of energy, enthusiasm, and time to send your demo CD to a small indie label as it will to reach the head of Sony Music.

But there's one caveat: If your music is perfectly matched to that small indie label, but totally inappropriate for Sony, stick with the indie label. There are always times to take risks and reach higher, but if you do your research, you'll know there's *very little* chance Sony Music is looking for a Swiss yodeling artist who plays the bongo drums. Their goal is to reach a large, mass market. Your yodeling may be fantastic, but it's probably not going to have the reach they need. Make the effort, but be sure you're approaching the right buyer.

Close the Deal

Everyone's on your side. They loved the pitch and they've been singing your praises for half an hour. Now it's time to get down to business. This is where the abstract "sell" becomes concrete. This is where you're asking for money, an opportunity, a contract—whatever it is you want to take away from the whole process. And the key word here is asking.

In my experience, most women have a mental block when it comes to asking. We're taught to please, to make friends, and to make sure everyone else—from the guy foaming our latte to a mean-spirited coworker—is happy before we take care of ourselves. Asking is an art. Here's what you need to know.

It gets easier with practice.

Try it on neutral territory. Ask for discounts when you shop. Ask for a better table in your favorite restaurant. Ask friends to meet closer to your office, rather than eighteen subway stops down the line. Ask for assignments at work. Ask to meet people. The more you do it, the easier and more fun it becomes. And this is the great part—it really does become fun. The world starts opening up to you.

Make targeted requests.

For example, asking for "help" likely will get you enthusiasm without a lot of action. Why? People need the specifics. Asking someone to proofread, make specific phone calls, or track down certain information will be far more effective. Also, you don't want to waste people's time. The more specific you are, the less time and effort they need to invest, and the more likely they are to agree. Lay out your request clearly and quickly. The simpler the better.

Get some perspective.

Head off your fear by putting yourself in the other person's shoes. Are you asking for their firstborn? A waterfront home? I'm guessing no. In many cases, your request will be simple and the other person may be happy to accommodate your needs. On the other side, a "No" likely has nothing to do with you. It's probably about budgets, time, energy, effort, or established realities for the person on the other hand. The truth? You need to have a thick skin if you're going to take risks and make requests.

Nobody's doing it.

Asking will set you apart. Not only will you be 100 percent more likely to get what you want, it will actually make you look better. You look competent and you'll boost your value, even if the person/company/client on the other end says no. They'll respect you simply for asking.

NEGOTIATION

Once you get down to asking, you're entering a brave new phase—negotiation. And let's face it. Negotiation is a word that makes most people's hair stand on end. There's something about hammering out the details that makes the best of us want to run for the door. But negotiation is critical. It's your chance to walk away with a great contract, a job that has fair pay *and* medical benefits, or a business deal that will keep your doors open and your fridge stocked with food.

On the heels of a tough negotiation in my business, I started to think about the process—and how to make it feel more straightforward, more interesting, and most importantly, more *doable*. I came to realize that negotiation is just like dating. As we move step-by-step through the negotiation process, pull out your little black book and follow along.

The Meeting

Your eyes lock across a crowded room. The music is thumping. The room is packed. You're wearing your best shoes, your best dress, and you're feeling fine. Your buyer's looking pretty hot, too. He sidles over and offers you a drink. You start to flirt. You make small talk. Everything's fun, upbeat, and exciting. Your pulse races a little as you swap business cards and head home (separately) for the night. *Could this job be the one? Is the deal going to turn the company around? Am I finally going to land that breakthrough film role?*

After the meeting, you fall asleep with a head full of possibility.

The Callback

Ah, the callback. There's no denying that you had chemistry. There's mutual interest. But who makes the first call—and how quickly do you dial those digits? It's a delicate balance. Too soon, and you'll scare off your buyer. Too late, and you may lose the opportunity. He could have spotted someone else or decided that it's not worth all the effort. This is where the straight-up fun and rush of excitement becomes just a little bit stressful.

If the interview/meeting or initial discussion was amazing, don't hesitate to send that thank-you note or follow up with a quick e-mail. The key is to keep it light. You enjoyed meeting your buyer—say so. Add a shared joke, a personal detail, and move on. If he's not into you, what can you do? Don't take it personally, and get back out there in your finest threads. Someone else will be thrilled to make a deal.

The First Date

He called! You've landed the interview, the formal pitch, or an exploratory meeting with the head of acquisitions. You're going on a first date. Now it's time to prepare. Wear something fun, yet professional. You mean business, but you still want to feel comfortable. Remember that this is just a first date. He could turn out to be a stalker, or a workaholic, or, worse yet—maybe he still lives with his mom. Remember that, as much as you want to shine, you're still in size-up mode. He's got to fit the bill, too.

You start to ask lightly probing questions: *Do you have a big family?* (Translation: Do you like children?) *How long has your team worked together?* (Is this a good office environment?) You're assessing your buyer without tackling the tough issues straight on. Because really, neither of you will want to take this further if you're not well matched. You're looking for deal-breakers and so is he. Keep it fun, but don't talk yourself into having a good time. If the fit is right, the hours will feel like minutes and you'll linger over dessert, then a coffee, then another coffee . . .

Getting Serious

You've been dating—exchanging calls, hanging out, getting to know each other better—and it's starting to get serious. Maybe you've met each other's friends (team, partners, staff) and you're starting to get attached. You think this could be something real. On those rare days when he doesn't call, you realize that you miss him. You're both getting more invested. You want to see this work.

Maybe you've been back for a second or third interview, you've exchanged proposals back and forth, or you've shown your work to the gallery manager, owner, and a group of top clients. The attraction level is high and you hit new milestones together. Surrender yourself to the experience, but make sure you're still happy with how things are going. Make sure you're both in the driver's seat, and that you're heading in a direction that fits with your needs and values.

The Commitment Talk

It happens late one night over drinks, a sober afternoon coffee, or maybe in the warm glow of the morning after. *Where's this going? Are we ready to commit? Is it time to stop seeing other people?* The commitment talk can either be incredibly gratifying or scary and claustrophobic. You've got to proceed cautiously and carefully.

This is where you start to work out the terms. *Will we move in together? Will I work from the Chicago or the Atlanta office? Can you offer me $100,000 to start? Will you handle promotions for this event or is it my responsibility?* The toughest part lies in getting it started. It's scary to make the first move, but someone has to take a deep breath and start talking. Sure, you'll feel vulnerable, but there's too much at stake to stay quiet. Whether you're talking money, benefits, hours, or shipping, do your research and be ready to talk numbers and specifics. Then it becomes a tennis match, with details (and counteroffers) hit back and forth across the net.

The commitment talk can last mere minutes, or it can extend into days, weeks, or months. It all depends on you and your partner. Remember that this is the moment when you have to be brutally honest. Can you live with these terms? It's time to speak up or move on. This is your chance to get what you want—and to ensure you're buyer is thrilled with the outcome as well.

The Proposal

The offer takes you by surprise after a romantic dinner. *Will you marry me? The job is yours if you want it. We want to represent you in the gallery. We're ready to sign the paperwork.* Your heart is racing. You're sweating and thinking a million thoughts at once. It's the moment of truth, and there are three ways this could go.

Scenario One, you say yes and live happily ever after. The deal is right, your partner's perfect, and you're happy with the relationship exactly as it is. Two, you're not ready yet. Sure, you're in love and you want to stay together, but the terms aren't quite right. You can't sign on the dotted line without a few changes. You'll end up having the commitment talk again down the road, and you'll rehash details. And this is a smart step. If you don't feel in your heart that it's right, don't seal the deal. Scenario Three, you say no. Despite all the talking and planning and time, you realize that this just isn't the buyer for you. Something has been telling you to walk away, and ultimately, you feel relieved when you return his things and decide the wedding's off.

This is it. Negotiation. If you don't get to this point, you're not going to get anywhere. You're not going to get your *more*. Most people are scared of this point—and who can blame them? Negotiating makes you vulnerable. It means you could get hurt. But like everything worth doing in life, you've got to stand up straight and go for it. You won't have a life partner if you can't commit. If you've decided you want a serious, long-term relationship but you're spending every night curled up on the couch in your sweats, good luck. You have to dance the dance. Get out there, meet your buyer, and start drawing up the fine print. Make your sale and put it in writing. Negotiation is one of the best skills to master, so keep practicing. Just like dating, it gets easier with time—and no matter how many times your heart has been broken, you will make the deal of a life-time. It just takes patience, commitment, and a high level of self-understanding.

In the next section, we're going to cover "the personal touch"—using the best of yourself to make your negotiations and your sales process more fun, more interesting, and ultimately, more effective.

THE PERSONAL TOUCH

I'm sitting in my office. I can barely see over the files, books, and empty coffee cups scattered on my desk, so I'm not too thrilled when the courier arrives. "What now?" I think, as I rip open the package. What do I find? A black, coil-bound sketchbook and a pretty, hand-written note. As I flip through the pages, I find a painstaking collection of potential outfits—tops, skirts, pants, shoes, boots, jewelry—clipped from magazines and arranged into different "looks." All are beautiful, and a hands-down match with my personal style. The whole thing must have taken hours, even days, to create.

I read the note. It's from Jennine, a young woman who worked as a makeup artist on our television show. We had been chatting on set about my upcoming book tour, and how I was overwhelmed by the idea of pulling together not one, but six, weeks' worth of fabulous Wildly Sophisticated outfits. I picked up the phone and called her on the spot.

I love telling this story, because it has to be the best example I've ever seen of using your personal touch to ensure a "sale"—even when there isn't anything on the market to start with! I wasn't planning on hiring a stylist. I was counting on bribing my best friend, Jenn, with coffee and lunch to hit the stores with me. But Jennine went so far above and beyond, and she was so on-target with my sense of style, that I hired her that day.

Not only had Jennine shown incredible initiative, she had listened, really listened, that afternoon on the set, and she made her "pitch" with my needs in mind. She didn't have to push her own talents because her fashion sense already jumped off the page. When we're constantly bombarded by pushy sales tactics, it's amazing when someone gives you exactly, and authentically, what you need.

> *Next time you're working on a sales proposal, learn as much as you can about the person you're pitching to, and create a package that personalizes your sale.*

Ask yourself, what specific skills, talents, or products can you add that will make your pitch more memorable?

Start with thank-you notes. In this age of e-mail and voice messaging, sending a hand-written thank-you note is one of the simplest, most effective ways of setting yourself apart from the pack, and moving that much closer to a sale. Never underestimate the power of expressing your heartfelt thanks for an offer or an opportunity. But don't stop there. Whenever you're in a sales situation, think of how you can personalize the pitch and use yourself to meet, and exceed, your customer's expectations. Do make sure the personal touch fits the situation, however. Home-baked cookies probably aren't the most professional bonus—unless you're a baker, or you're up for a catering gig. Ensure you personalize your pitch with something situation-appropriate.

Photocopy salesperson, makeup artist, skydiving instructor, veterinarian, chef—I don't care who you are or what business you're in, your ability to sell is going to make the difference between

dreaming about your more and actually living it. We all need to sell ourselves in order not only to earn what we're worth, but, as you'll learn in the next chapter, to create our own terms.

wildly sophisticated icons

❋ Melanie Dunea

Freelance photographer

Melanie's portfolio is jam-packed with rich, expressive portraits that capture not just an image, but the essence of the person in front of her lens. She's shot all the big names: Sting, Colin Farrell, Heath Ledger, Rudolph Giuliani, Sir Ian McKellen. Melanie does portrait work, editorial photography, and Fall 2004, she and photographer Nigel Parry released a striking collection titled *Precious.* The couple is donating all royalties from the book to the Starlight Children's Foundation—an international nonprofit organization dedicated to improving the equality of life for seriously ill children and their families.

A Chicago native, Melanie worked briefly as a photojournalist in France, then spent her twenties learning the ropes as a photo assistant. She eventually struck out on her own and is currently represented by the prestigious CPi agency. Thanks to a sharp eye and a gracious, fun-loving spirit, Melanie has a thriving, globe-trotting career in one of the world's toughest markets—New York City.

What does your work mean to you?
Passion. Absolute passion. If I'm not shooting, I get depressed. It's like food. Taking pictures. Photography is a way of life, not a job. In fact, I can't even say, "I'm going to work today."

What's the best investment you've ever made?
It's a very ongoing investment in self-promotion. That's the number one key to photography, and it's an incredible investment because it's ongoing. You

need to keep knocking on people's doors, seeing them, calling them and sending them new work. I started with one portfolio and now I have twenty.

How much time do you spend on self-promotion?

For a freelancer, self-promotion is a nonstop challenge. The minute that I leave a photo shoot, I should be on the phone. You're only as good as your last picture, and you should be out there calling. And if you're not calling, you should be out at the newsstands looking for new magazines. Looking for new places to send your book. Following up with people. Touching base. If you're not working, and you're not promoting yourself, then you're not going to keep working.

What is the greatest lesson you've learned about your work and the business of photography?

As a freelancer, your work comes and goes. I call it the wave. You're at the top one minute and you're falling down the next. It's a cycle. I try to work on not getting down on myself when the cycle is at the bottom. When the phone isn't ringing and I'm not shooting right through the weekend, through holidays, I have to remember that there are natural ups and downs. You can't be up all the time, and if you were, then you wouldn't be driven. That's a great lesson, and I'm still learning it.

What's the best financial advice you've ever received?

Don't overcommit yourself. I think that's very important because there are so many hidden expenses. Let's say you're shooting somebody fabulous and then you're out for dinner. Who's going to pay for that? Not the fabulous person. So, I think not overcommitting yourself is key. You have to bear so many hidden costs and you have to be prepared for when a great opportunity does arise, so that you can finance it.

⁕ Jamie Salé

Professional figure skater

We all watched as Jamie and her partner, David Pelletier, skated their way to silver, then gold, at the 2002 Winter Olympics in Salt Lake City. The pair gained greater notoriety for their reluctant role in the Olympic judging scandal, but they also amazed legions of fans by handling the situation with utter grace and dignity.

The Olympics may have marked the first time the *whole world* sat up and took notice of Jamie's flawless technique, on-ice artistry, and exuberant smile, but this Canadian-born athlete has been skating since she was five years old. That means mornings, afternoons, and evenings at the rink, and a life-long commitment to her sport. Now a professional skater, Jamie tours the world, performing with David—her partner on the ice and off.

What does money mean to you?
Stability. I know that I will not have to worry. But, it's really material—it's just material stuff. What makes me happy is what I do with my life and the people that I surround myself with. Going to hockey games or spending the afternoon with my girlfriends or having coffee. Those are the things that make me happy. I've got lots of money now, but it's not important. My mom and I always say, "You know, things were really good when we had nothing." I mean, we had to use patio furniture for our kitchen table, but we had just the best times. You make your own happiness and you make it with what you have.

What's the best investment you've ever made?
Waiting to skate with David [Pelletier] was the best investment I've ever made. I had a previous partner, and we had done fairly well, but I had always wanted to skate with Dave. I had my eyes on him for a long time, and I just kept hoping and persevering and waiting. At that point, I was just doing singles and it wasn't going very far. You can't even imagine some of the comments people made and what they said about me. I don't know how I stuck with it, but I did. A few years later, I found out that he was going to quit skating, and I said,

"You can't. I've been waiting to skate with you for years." Waiting was my investment—emotionally and financially. And now, I have such an incredible life.

How important is image and self-promotion in your career?
What really makes a difference is how you treat people. You have to treat everybody equally. My "product" on the ice speaks for itself, but I also want to have a career off the ice as well. You want to be known as personable and someone who is easy to talk to, and fun. Most people don't really know me. They just know my image. I had this image as the cute figure-skating Canadian with the ponytail and this wholesome little girl. So, when *FHM* magazine called and asked me to pose for the magazine, I thought, "How could I turn this down?"

I went out on a limb and tried something new, and okay, there will always be people who don't understand my chores. People who can only see me as I am on the ice. But I also opened a lot of people's eyes. It was a new opportunity, and I always think, Why not? Would you turn that opportunity down?

8

How Do I Create My Own Terms?

Drawing the Line Between Debt and Investment in Your Career

I can't even tell you how many times I'd be sitting in a meeting, driving into the office, or signing on another dotted line, and think, "I've either got this all together, or I am totally and completely screwed."

In these moments of confusion, despair, and absolute exhilaration, all I wanted was an answer. Have I gone too far? Is it time to give up? Or is this simply what it takes to succeed?

I looked everywhere. I asked my accountant and my investors. I scoured the bookshelves. I immersed myself in budgets. I even consulted a tea-leaf reader. And while I still hold desperately to her vision that what I'm creating is going to "take off like a shooting star," I've come to understand that no one could tell me whether my business was a debt or an investment.

Very slowly, very painfully, and eventually, very contentedly, I realized I had to create my own terms.

The nature of risk, the ability to build a dream, the reality of creating more with your life requires both debt and investment, and on any given day, the same situation can swing back and forth between the two.

The line between debt and investment is one of the most frightening, exciting, excruciating, and, quite frankly, the most exhilarating places to be. And this is the most important thing to know—experiencing this line is *absolutely* necessary to create wealth. How do you make yourself comfortable in one the most uncomfortable of places?

Create your own terms.

I've spoken with women around the country and, not only are debt and investment two of the scariest words around, the majority of us can't figure out what's what, regardless of the fact that everyone seems ready to offer advice:

> "Buy low, sell high. Stay clear of debt at any cost. Put six months' worth of living expenses into a savings account. Now's the time to take the risk, take your savings and invest in your dream. Renting your home is like flushing cash down the toilet."

Common sense money rules are everywhere you turn. There's just one problem. Our lives and our careers are not one-size-fits-all.

When I think about this chapter and the fact that you're soon to be taking what you've learned to the marketplace to create your *more,* I want you to be crystal clear that it's through the process of creating your own terms that you truly experience success.

I'm also acutely aware that as an artist, a teacher, a PR agent, a web designer, a doctor—whatever—you might be thinking, "What do debt and investment mean to my career?" These concepts are not just for entrepreneurs or bankers. Understanding the essence of what nurtures you (investment) and what depletes you (debt) is crucial for making decisions in your career.

This chapter will focus on redefining judgment-laden words like *debt* and *investment*. You'll quickly learn that one woman's debt is another woman's rock-solid investment. What's the difference? It's all about how you feel. Then, we'll explore the power of choice. Investment or debt? Beyond the technical definition, the answer to this question comes down to a handful of feelings and a very important and very personal choice.

Throw out the textbooks and get ready to redefine money, wealth, risk, and investment—on your own terms.

IT'S ALL PERSONAL

Debt, investment, money, risk—it's all personal. And it can feel really frustrating when your career and your values don't fit into a nice, neat little package. When your life exists in total opposition to every financial guidebook on the shelves, it's hard not to feel like you're doing something wrong.

While I'm not sure if this is going to make you feel better or worse, when it comes to your money and your career, there is no right or wrong. There are only choices. Your goal is not to become a textbook case for Finance 101. Instead, your Number One Responsibility is to ensure that your choices reflect your values and your goals. That's why it's so important to create your own terms—with your money, with your life, and with your career.

I was asked the other day, "What is the best investment you've ever made?" Looking back, I immediately knew what my answer was, but, at the time, it could just as easily have been considered a debt. Several years ago, I was only starting to build my business and I was exploring the world of publishing. I had to learn about literary agents from scratch, and the prospect of writing a one-page letter describing my book, my business, and my passion for young women and work seemed more than a little daunting. I completed the whole query-letter process, and, with a handful of positive responses, the next question was: Who? Who did I want to represent this book? I was living on the other side of the country, and, at that point, *Sex and the City* was the closest I'd ever been to the Big Apple. I couldn't help wishing that I lived closer to the action so we could meet for lunch or a coffee and I could get a gut feel for whom I most wanted to work with.

With the vast majority of my savings already invested in my business, I looked to my credit card. Now, let's be honest, this wasn't the first time I had considered credit to get what I *wanted*. But this case was different. I very consciously decided this would be the tool I would use to get what I *needed*. I was going to fly myself to New York for a week. At that time in my life, a thousand bucks felt like a million. Dipping into my credit was one part brilliance, one part lunacy.

And this is the point. The most challenging and confusing part of examining debt and investment is that your choices can be both—even at the same time. And worse, you don't know if you're staring down a debt or an investment until all the pieces are in place and the situation is wrapped up.

> To gain what is worth having, it may be necessary to lose everything else.
> —Bernadette Devlin

I went into debt to travel to New York. But upon meeting, and now, working with my agent for the last several years, it was the best investment I've ever made.

Let's look at the basics of debt versus investment.

DEBT VERSUS INVESTMENT

Debt

The dictionary defines debt as: "a state of owing or obligation." And obligation is: "the act of obliging one to a course of action, as by a promise or a vow." The owing part is simple. If you borrow money from the bank, you owe them the amount of cash you borrowed, plus interest (their reward for lending it to you in the first place). In simple terms, you are obliged to return that money. You've signed a contract and agreed to a course of action that includes full repayment. Your loan is, technically, a debt.

Common financial wisdom suggests that debt is undesirable. It means that someone else has a claim on your money, and that state of owing is something everyone should avoid. But if you're going to school, building your career, growing your business, or taking great risks in your life and work, debt is often not only unavoidable, it's smart. Consider these two scenarios:

Scenario A

It's 3 A.M. You can't sleep. You're too busy worrying about your credit card bills. You haven't even opened the worst one. Too thick to fit in the customary envelope, they've thrown it into an 8½-by-11-inch package, and it's still sitting on the kitchen table. You've done *waaaay* too much shopping this month and now you're suffering. You feel guilty. You're embarrassed. In this case, your credit card bill is a debt—financially, emotionally, personally. It has obliged you to a course of action—paying for things you may not actually want or need—that isn't consistent with who you are or what you value. That bulging statement is not only frightening, it's draining your self-confidence.

Scenario B

Again, 3 A.M. You can't sleep. You're too excited about starting med school tomorrow. You had to put the first semester's tuition on your credit card, but you've got a plan. You're a little concerned about paying the bills in time to fund your second semester, but you've thought it through and it feels good. You're proud of yourself. Diving in took guts, and you know you're on the right track. Your credit card statement is a debt, financially speaking, but it has obliged you to a course of action—getting your medical degree, which makes you feel strong and smart. Emotionally and personally, that debt just became an investment.

In order to create anything of significant value, to reach for, and to obtain, your more, please know you're going to experience some kind of debt. But it's not all about your bank account. In deciding if something is worth investing in, you really do need to consider the implications for your sleep, your health, and your relationships.

Sleep Debt

It's not even just the string of late nights and early mornings necessary for creating your more, it's the stress that haunts you in the wee hours of the night. The sleep deprivation I've experienced over the last three years has been a huge debt in my life. I'll pick up Cheri in the morning, my eyes still half shut, yawning at every stoplight, and I'll ask, "So, how was your sleep?"

"Great!" she answers, with so much enthusiasm she jolts me out of my stupor. I've gone to great lengths to get as much shut-eye as possible. I won't let even a drop of liquid past my lips after 7 P.M., for fear of waking up at 3 A.M., my mind activated and whirling in the dark for the next four hours as I imagine every disastrous possibility for my life. Sleep deprivation really is a debt. Without sleep, you're simply not as sharp, as fully able to make decisions, and to gain perspective on everything around you.

How to manage sleep debt.

Other than Cheri, I don't know too many people who haven't encountered a little difficulty with Mr. Sandman, thanks to the stress attached to investment or debt. Whether you're getting married next week, you're starting your first course, or you're making a big presentation, you may encounter difficulty laying down your head and resting your mind. This is normal, and if you haven't experienced months of deprivation, it's nothing a relaxing bath before bed or a strong cup of coffee first thing in the morning isn't going to fix. In the case of short-term sleepless nights, the best thing you can do for yourself is to understand that it's par for the course. Don't get too worked up about it. Stressing out about your lack of sleep will make you cycle into a more serious problem. It's after you've watched Letterman and you're half afraid to turn off the light in anticipation of another sleepless night that you start to move into the danger zone. The anxiety of sleeplessness will keep you further away from REM than almost anything else.

If your sleep has been disrupted for weeks and your sleeping pattern has been knocked seriously off-kilter, you might need some help. Go visit your doctor and talk with her about your sleeplessness. Major disruption in sleep patterns can be indicative of more significant illnesses. If not, your doctor can prescribe a nonaddictive sleep aid that will help you get back into a regular pattern.

Sleep deprivation not only can pinpoint an illness, but it has this uncanny way of telling you when you might be paying too high a price. While you can tell yourself a million times that the shit job, the business loan, or the eighty hours a week is worth the investment, your body (a very authentic and reliable gauge) may be suggesting otherwise.

Physical Debt

The focus, attention, and drive needed for investment has the potential to have serious repercussions on your physical health. First and foremost, you have might have the "high-alert" body. Every nerve ending's throbbing, your head is pounding, your adrenaline pumping—you're in a constant state of "readiness." You're poised to pounce or be pounced on, and being in this state for extended periods of time will put you into physical debt.

The other aspect of physical debt comes with the fact that you've been so invested in creating your business plan, finishing that grueling graduate degree in architecture, or designing that website, that your pulse has flatlined from a total lack of physical activity. Over and over again, I work with women who are so invested in their success that they've let their physical health go by the wayside. Chocolate-bar dinners and decades-old athletic wear that still includes leg warmers are sure indicators that you're moving into physical debt.

How to manage physical debt.
I, too, let my whole body atrophy with the thought that there was no way I had time to work out, but I was so wrong. All it took was one run to figure this out. I came back to the office sore but nevertheless restored, vitalized, and inspired to work harder. In reality, taking the time to work out for an

hour three times a week increases your production tenfold. When you're investing, you absolutely need a sense of priority and perspective. Really, Kate Hudson didn't lose those seventy-five pounds of baby weight in what looked like three weeks by happenstance. That was a full-time job, not only for her, but for her trainer and chef. Most of us don't have that kind of luxury, but that's not what I'm talking about, anyway. I'm referring to keeping your body in motion. Start to walk, run, cycle—whatever you enjoy.

While I'm all about resting that high-energy body we talked about, in my experience, motion is the key to blowing off some steam and getting a real sense of release. Exercise is a way of getting the whirl out of your head and body and into the water at the pool, the wind that follows you as you cycle, or the pavement you pound with each step. You can exercise out some of that nervous energy that comes with high-stakes investment. We talked about this in our intangible section; your physical health is directly connected to your sense of worthiness, and physical debt will keep you at arm's length from your more.

Social Debt

My friend Kel is an Ironman triathlete, and as much as she loves to eat and drink with her friends, when she's on a training schedule, not only is she in bed by 9 P.M., but, unless we're shimmying up to the bar for a shot of wheatgrass, she's out. It sucks. She hates it, but she's invested. She misses us, but her one-hundred-mile bike ride is a long way for us to drive, let alone, pedal along beside her. She has to the pay the price of lonely training sessions in the pool and solitary sunrise runs, but that's what her investment requires.

While your investment may not look anything like a fifteen-hour physical event, the reality is, it's likely to require some form of social or relationship debt. Your decision to take that travel-oriented dream job keeps you away from your husband, the promotional transfer to Boston keeps you away from your family, or that picture you're painting in the isolated cottage up in the Catskills keeps you away from civilization. When you're committing everything you've got toward your investment, you're inevitably going to experience some form of social debt.

How to manage social debt.

"So, how do you deal with friends who keep on pushing for time?" asked Kel, on one rare afternoon together during her training season. One of the most inspiring and motivating experiences I've had was at the finish line of one of Kelly's races. Her expression of joy, exhaustion, and relief, as she broke through the threshold, was extraordinary.

"Why don't you get copies of the picture of you crossing the finish line and write some notes to explain what you're doing and why you're doing it," I suggested. "Ask everyone for patience and express your excitement at seeing them all again after the race." Making people a part of your investment and helping them to understand why it's so important to you will go a long way toward keeping your social debt down. The other thing to remember is

> Life is short, and it is here to be lived.
>
> —Kate Winslet

that, often when you're committing sixty hours a week to a new job, business, or intensive project, you're going to form new relationships based upon circumstance. You might find some new amazing social circles.

One of the greatest things that come from times of intensive investment that make demands on your social network is that you get a view into who your real friends are. If your friend Beth, as much as you've explained what you're up to, keeps badgering you in a guilt-provoking kind of way, it's her problem, not yours.

The Ultimate Debt

Before we move on to investment, take a second to think about what I call "the ultimate debt." What is it? Looking back on your life and saying, "I wish I had . . ." I can't think of a heavier, more heart-wrenching debt. Kind of blows those business loans out of the water, doesn't it?

INVESTMENT

Now let's look at the definition of investment: "committing money in order to earn a financial return, or to make use of for future benefits and advancements." You can substitute for the word *money* whatever it is you're putting on the line—your time, your energy, your determination.

Here's the interesting part. Even if we were talking about the exact same amount of money, those two sleepless, credit-card-stress scenarios we laid out earlier feel radically different. The money committed to an M.B.A. program will help you achieve future benefits and advancements. In my book, the credit card bill is a debt, but that medical degree is an investment, no question. And how you feel is what's most important. The technical reality of owing money can either limit or free you. Your financial choices will weigh you down, or give you the ability to do what you want and need to do. When you understand the difference, it's easier to ignore all the experts and make decisions that work well, and feel right, for you.

RETURN ON INVESTMENT

In any investment scenario, it all comes down to what you're getting from all those grueling hours, your tremendous efforts, and your sacrifices. A home on a far-off island, retirement at thirty, your face on the cover of *Fortune* magazine . . . What will be your return on investment?

Maybe it's the moment when you know your life "fits" a little better. It's more money. It's more joy throughout your day. It's the ability to decide when you're working and when you're playing. Reward is the carrot dangling on the end of the stick. Reward is what drives you to work a little harder, save your cash for a down payment, or make that big career move you've been thinking and dreaming about for so long. Everyone is chasing their own, unique set of rewards—their *more*.

One of our favorite questions to ask all our Wildly Sophisticated Icons we interviewed for this book was, "What is the best investment you've ever made?" Initially, we thought we'd hear stories of investment property, interview suits, PR agents, and high-level courses. Instead, each and every woman we interviewed answered the question with a variation of this response: *Myself*.

This is the key. You and your career are the single most important thing you need to be continually investing in. If you're questioning whether an opportunity is a good investment, here are a few of the things that, in my experience, always generate great rewards.

Opportunities that will differentiate you.

How many people do you know who have studied in Africa, sung in a band, or competed in a marathon? If your investment results in an opportunity to ensure you stand out from the crowd, go for it. Being unique is a key strategy for creating more.

Meeting face-to-face.

I am a firm believer that an opportunity to let someone see you, feel your energy, and allow you to communicate your passion in person is always a great return on your investment. When there's a lot at stake, it's tough to put yourself across on a phone line or in an application. You lose visual and physical cues that help to build relationships. If at all possible, request the opportunity to meet someone face-to-face.

Learning will help you to create more.

Learning is one of the most long-lasting and important returns you can get from any investment. On a small scale, are you considering a two-hundred-dollar wine course? Just imagine how many times you'll be able to make an intelligent recommendation from the menu. On a larger scale, your graduate degree might open doors that are difficult to enter.

Opportunities to put your money where your mouth is.
There's a lot of hot air out there in the world of work. Any opportunity to actually show you've got what it takes is a return that will pay incredible dividends—not only to your own bank of confidence, but to those who are wondering if you're worth it.

One last thing before we move into the next section. Hating a job that pays well is NEVER a good investment strategy. Not only have I lived this monumental mistake myself, I've seen many of my friends and coworkers struggle in the same trap. I've come to learn that those who hate their well-paying jobs spend a phenomenal amount of money compensating. Food, clothes, vacations—all absolute necessities for someone who hates what they do for a living. I swear, those who hate their jobs actually take home less money.

> There are people who have money and people who are rich.
>
> —Coco Chanel

WHY RISK AN INVESTMENT?

There are two ways to increase your financial status: save the cash you've got, or make more of it. Those who are not afraid of debt believe in two things:

- Their capacity to *make more*

- Their capacity to *recover*

The reality of your grandma putting her last $200,000 of retirement savings into a high-risk start-up is a much different scenario than you bucking up the cash at an early point in your career. Even with the best of attitudes, Grandma doesn't have another thirty years in the job market to make it back. You do. If you're making an investment decisions now, here's why you've got an age advantage:

You've got more time to recover
You're twenty-two, twenty-eight, thirty-two. You're just getting started.

You're less likely to have dependents
Beyond ensuring Buster, the dog, has food in his bowl, at this stage, I'm as-suming you're not responsible for a family of five.

It's easier to start over, get back into the job market, change course, and redefine yourself
The average person changes jobs six to ten times in their career. If you take a nosedive, no one is going to question your change in direction, and you have plenty of years left to apply what you've learned from the situation.

People will respect your risks and judge you less harshly when you're young
Brutal, and not exactly politically correct, but true.

Here's a little hint in the risk/investment department. If you've been sitting on a decision for a long time, if it haunts you, if you've gotten to the point of obsession—it's time. And let me tell you, we're talking both per-sonal and professional risks. How many days in a row have you questioned whether this relationship still works? How many times have you woken up in the night knowing you need to talk with your boss about a sabbatical? How often do you look at other people in the airport, in the street, on the subway, and think, "Their life is better than mine?" How many times do you walk down the street dreaming of how your life would change if you actually started that business or took that trip to Asia?

THE POWER OF CHOICE

Have you ever been moving in a direction without consciously making a choice? It's not like you didn't decide. At some point, you put yourself in motion, but you're not exactly sure when, and you can't remember why. I had already decided to create Wildly Sophisticated Media, in fact, I had decided on numerous occasions, but at one very challenging point in the business—when I could have given up or I needed to recommit in order to move forward—I had to make a fully conscious choice to reinvest myself.

In the end, that choice was one of the most important ways I have created more success for myself and my business. That choice to persevere was an investment. Some people may have thought I was crazy to continue, but by sitting down and choosing, and fully embracing, my decision, I gathered the strength to handle everything that would come along. The act of choosing made me feel infinitely more invested, prepared, and driven.

In most cases, choice is the difference between debt and investment. Choice is conscious. Choice is proactive. Choice is empowering. Choice is responsible. Choice, by virtue of its inherent power, inspires action, perseverance, and passion—everything you need to create success. There are three primary pieces to the choice process:

Examine All Potential Options

Choice is so much easier, once you have a handle on all the potential options and you've got a clear sense of what it will actually take to succeed. I was in a presentation at a prestigious college, and toward the end of our session, a young woman put up her hand and asked, "I'm thinking about either getting my master's in English literature or becoming a wedding planner. What do you think is my best choice?" I had to ask: What do you know about being a wedding planner? Her response? "I saw the Jennifer Lopez movie and it looked so exciting." My suggestion? You can't make a decision of this magnitude with a flick as your frame of reference.

Choices are best made with a solid sense of what you're actually committing to and why. On the road of investment, there will be many points at which you wonder whether you've made the right decision. Reviewing *all* your options before you make a choice will give you a stronger sense of determination and the confidence to know you're on the right path.

Consider Your Worst-Case Scenario

"It all comes down to envisioning your worst-case scenario and deciding if you can live with it." This advice comes straight from a former risk assessor for PricewaterhouseCoopers. Consider, "What's the worst that can happen?" Ask this question from both sides of the fence—taking action and choosing not to jump. For example, "I could go bankrupt, or I could be eigthty, sitting on a porch feeling resentful and wondering 'What if'."

Go Back to Your Values

You worked so hard on your value assessment for a reason. In the face of multiple choices, this is what it all comes down to. Are you going to invest in a move to New York to audition on Broadway at the expense of your relationship with your boyfriend? It depends what you value—and yes, you've got to consider what you value *more*. Again, it all comes down to choices. A decision to move may not mean that you don't love or value your boyfriend, but don't kid yourself into thinking things won't have the potential to change. Choosing one thing over another takes some tough deliberation, but it's often a crucial step.

> Think like a queen. A queen is not afraid to fail. Failure is another stepping-stone to greatness.
>
> —Oprah Winfrey

You've also got to consider your short-term versus long-term values. This is especially true of your money. You may decide to accept a low-paying internship, make an expensive move to a bigger city, book a flight on your credit card to meet face-to-face with an icon in your industry. Sometimes it may look like you don't value money—you're making a short-term decision to have less money—with the intention of making more.

DEPRIVATION VERSUS SACRIFICE

Sacrifice: destruction or surrender of something for the sake of something else.

Deprive: to take something away from, or to withhold something from.

I've watched my friend Valerie go through a totally tumultuous breakup over the last couple of months, and, in listening to her, I've come to more clearly understand the difference between deprivation and sacrifice.

So to make a way-too-long story short, Valerie had decided it was time. She was going to leave her fiancé of five years. It had been a surprisingly long time coming. Almost as soon as he proposed, she was vaguely aware of a sense of dread, of the feeling that something wasn't quite right. Her family and friends delighted, the wedding registry chosen, her biological clock ticking, she pushed down her feelings of "Maybe I shouldn't" for years. And then the fateful day arrived. With what she described as a feeling of "There has to be something more," she decided it was time to sacrifice the relationship.

That was, of course, until he agreed. Yes, he agreed. In a fit of "Oh my God, what have I done?" she tried to convince him of all the reasons why this relationship might actually be worth salvaging. But he had already decided: He wasn't interested. All of sudden, Valerie's feeling of elation over her decision to sacrifice turned into a sad, fearful, sick feeling of deprivation. Exactly the same outcome, completely different experience.

When *she* chose, it was sacrifice, when *he* chose, it was deprivation.

Who hasn't had this kind of experience? Deciding to leave your job and being fired have the same outcome with completely different experiences attached. The reality is, human nature is such that we want what we can't have. This is an essential thing to remember in the face of choice around debt and investment.

It seems so obvious, but really, consciously considering the difference between deprivation

> **Without discipline, there's no life at all.**
> —Katharine Hepburn

and sacrifice is an incredible way not only to face a choice, but to ensure you can really live with it. The next time you decide to go without the latest Coach bag, the second piece of cake, or drinks with the girls, ask yourself: is this deprivation or sacrifice? There are a few ways to make your sacrifices just a little bit easier. Be prepared, and you'll be ahead of the game.

Keep your nose away from the glass.

When you've made a choice or a sacrifice and you need to exhibit self-control, stay away, far away, from your vice. If you've just started the Atkins diet, you really shouldn't meet your best friend for coffee at Krispy Kreme. If you've decided that you need to build more security and permanence in your job, don't hang out with a group of entrepreneurs or friends who are embarking on major career leaps. For now, surround yourself with people who are on a parallel path or who have achieved what you're trying to build.

Fuel your choices.

Let's say you just started working part-time in order to write your screenplay. Now you've got to watch your spending and stop ordering so much take-out. You're sacrificing some money and convenience in order to achieve a passionate personal goal. Fantastic. Feel good about your choice and then make it as doable as possible. Create a welcoming space for writing. Stock up on coffee, tea, or whatever beverage fuels your creativity—unless maybe that beverage is a gin martini. If the morning is your most productive time, go to bed early enough to rise and write. Smooth your own path and revel in the power of your choices.

> No matter how far life pushes you down, no matter how much you hurt, you can always bounce back.
> —Sheryl Swoopes

Get some perspective.

Sacrifice is all a matter of degree. While completing my last year at university, I spent a semester studying in Russia. On most days, the prospect of a hot shower was somewhere between slim and none. I came home after six weeks of jolting my body in and out of frigid water with an almost religious appreciation for hot showers. If you feel like giving up a new Gucci bag is tough stuff, you really need to give your head a shake. In North America, most of us barely know the meaning of deprivation. Remember that it's all relative.

Tune Out the Noise

Let's take the infamous coffee debate—is that morning cappuccino a debt or an investment? It depends. Does the thought of that coffee actually get you out of bed in the morning? Does it warm your hands and put a little caffeine kick in your step? Does it comfort you in light of the killer day ahead? Do you savor every drop? Investment is my call.

> When I get logical, and I don't trust my instincts—that's when I get in trouble.
>
> —Angelina Jolie

Relax. I'm not going to tell you that the key to saving is cutting out the coffee, or the magazines, or the nail polish. What I am going to do is ask you to think "value" before you spend. Sometimes an hour in the bath with the new issue of *Elle* is the difference between finishing that $50,000 proposal or not. I won't scold you or claim that debt is bad and that savings should only show up in your bank account. Debt and investment, heart-thumping, complex, and personal as they are, need to be considered in relationship to one another.

If your response to the suggestion to pay down more than your minimum credit card balance is "No shit," then join the club. Choice is the crucial difference between debt and investment: When you've got solid plans and a steely work ethic to back them up, sometimes dipping in the red is the difference between achieving your dreams and settling for less than success.

Here are some key indicators of investment or debt to help you decide whether to buy that latte—or spend the cash on a gym membership—or not.

Investments:

- **Bring you joy** Every time you sip a cup of coffee at your sunny kitchen table, you remember why you bought the apartment and took on a mortgage. You feel comforted and comfortable.

- **Give you energy** Craving some calm and balance, you signed up for a month of yoga classes. You've been thinking about it for a year or two, and now that you've made the commitment, you'll be there three times a week.

- **Boost your self-esteem** You saved $10,000 to get your business off the ground. Regardless of what happens, you feel proud of your own discipline and courage.

- **Help other people** Taking your grandparents out for lunch once a week takes time and, let's face it, a lot of patience. But you've learned all about life in the Depression, and you've developed a relationship that you'll always cherish.

- **Surround you with great people** You've had to spend more time training your (young and a little underqualified) assistant, but she's got vision, drive, and creativity. She brings great energy to the team and has incredible ideas.

- **Help you achieve your dreams** Pennies are tight, but you found the cash for a plane ticket to San Francisco. That company you've always admired has asked you to come for an interview. This is your chance.

- **Just feel "right"** Everyone thinks you're nuts, but you've taken three months of unpaid leave to travel through South America. It's something you just know you need to do.

Debts:

- **Encourage lies** Those pricey pants you put on credit are actually a little snug, and you really didn't need another black turtleneck.

When your boyfriend asks about your shopping trip, you lie and say you didn't buy anything. Now you're dreading the Visa statement.

- **Undermine your confidence and self-respect** That new car looked so hot in the showroom. And with no money down, how could you say no? But you're falling further behind on the payments, and every time you sit behind the wheel, you feel guilty, embarrassed, and just a little smaller.

- **Take without giving** Everyone's had "friends" who drain your cash, call daily with a new personal emergency, and insult your taste in everything from music to men. All you get in return is a headache.

- **Sap your energy** You took a part-time job in the evenings to supplement your cash flow. Now you're snoring at your desk and you snapped at your boss during a staff meeting. What's worse, your side gig doesn't even pay that much.

- **Limit your choices** You took on a new client, based on a friend's referral. She's totally high-maintenance, and insists on meeting three times a week. Thanks to her huge workload, you've been missing brunch with the girls, you can't seem to get to the gym, and you had to turn down another, more lucrative client.

- **Just feel "wrong"** Your friends were bugging you to go in on a timeshare in the Hamptons, so you finally gave in and paid your (nonrefundable) portion. Now you've got three major projects to finish by August and the place needs major renovations. Something told you not to get involved . . .

As much as I've had times when I've been desperate for answers—which explains the psychic, tea-leaf reader, and why I

read my horoscope with a fairly real sense of superstition—I've gradually realized that there are no objective "answers" about debt and investment.

Your choices are ongoing. They never end. And you have to constantly keep checking and rechecking your emotional pulse. Debt and investment can be tricky, but know that if you follow your gut, your instincts, and your values, your life will exist in the black, not the red.

There are no cut-and-dried answers, only choices.

Make your choices and don't look back.

wildly sophisticated icons

✳ Miae Lim

Restaurateur

It's a common story. Put yourself through college by working as a waitress, bartender, or hostess. What's uncommon—and downright remarkable—is using what you've learned from your part-time gigs to open two successful nightclubs and three critically-acclaimed restaurants before your thirty-fifth birthday.

Miae established her first nightclub, Solo, in 1996, and Big Wig—complete with 1950s hooded hairdryers—in 1998. After learning the ropes after dark, Miae turned exclusively to food. Now she owns Mirai Sushi, Japonais, and Ohba—three distinctive Chicago restaurants. Miae has an incredible tolerance for risk, killer business instincts, and a down-to-earth outlook on her life and career. Always ready for more learning and greater challenges, watch for big things from this culinary entrepreneur.

What drives you?

You can't achieve success just by doing what you like. You can't open a restaurant and say, "God, I really love furniture." Everything comes with it.

You have to deal with the plumber and the electrician and the chef and the managers and the servers and the trainees—the list goes on and on. You start to realize that your purpose is to make it *all* work.

What's the best investment you've ever made?
Financially speaking, when I bought my first condo. Mentally, the best investment I've ever made was finding time for myself. There were times when I tried to stay away from relationships because I wasn't ready to be involved and I knew that I had to stay focused on something. I said, "I'm going to invest my time in coming home and listening to my Nina Simone CD and writing down my thoughts or my to-do list," or writing down new concepts or ideas that I had. I was just investing in myself.

How do you feel about debt?
I think debt actually goes hand-in-hand with becoming more successful, because the more successful that you become, people want to lend you more and more money. So, if you're accumulating debt while moving forward, and you're creating more success for yourself, then I'd say that's good debt. But if something's not working, you have to know your boundaries. You have to know how far you can go into debt and how far you can take yourself out.

Do you have any advice to offer to other women?
If you don't feel you're moving up fast enough at work, and you feel that you have more value, reanalyze that value and look at your position. Then, look at other people. After you look at someone else who is, without a doubt, totally working her butt off, it's time to ask yourself, "How can I get there?"

You have to feel balanced in every aspect of your life. If I feel really good about myself, I surround myself with people who are extremely motivating and then it all starts coming together. And no matter how you slice it, you've got to make sacrifices. It's all self-motivation and sacrifice—and then you won't believe some of the things that will come to you.

✳ Cameron Tuttle
Author, entrepreneur

Born with a lust for life and the most wonderfully wicked sense of humor, Cameron would be the ultimate road-trip companion. Cameron started her path with a degree in English literature from Brown University, and a career in the New York publishing world.

Drawn to the open road, she soon realized her trips would make for great writing. Soon came the *Bad Girl's Guide to the Open Road,* then a full series of "bad girl" books, merchandise, clothing, and accessories. As president and CEO of Bad Girl Swirl, Inc., Cameron is redefining the image of author-as-entrepreneur.

Have you always known who and what the "bad girl" is?
No, absolutely not. It's funny, but no one is more surprised than I am about the incredible success of this concept and the fact that there are just so many bad girls out there. But part of my success comes from the fact that it's all been very organic. It hasn't been the product of a bunch of people sitting in a room saying, "We see an opportunity here—let's make some money!" It's just my quirky brain. And it was more about sharing my individual experiences as a "bad girl" and as a woman with other bad girls who are making their way through life.

Do you have a rescue fantasy?
My rescue fantasy is selling my screen rights for a million dollars. So, it's more about taking my creativity to the next level. It's me winning the creative lottery. It's not about someone else. I learned a long time ago that no one is going to come and save me. And that's okay.

What does money mean to you?
Money, to me, represents freedom. It represents the freedom to live my life the way that I want to, and the ability to live without underlying fear. I think most women have been there at some point. That point of wondering, "Am

I going to able to take care of myself at some stage in this lifetime?" But, in the end, having money gives you the confidence to take risks.

How do you feel about debt?

I love debt. I've had a long and committed relationship with debt. Many of us are raised to think debt is bad, and certainly there is good debt and there is bad debt. But as long as you have a smart and viable plan for generating revenue and paying off those credit cards, I think it's fine. And it takes a certain amount of guts—it really does. They don't call it "going for broke" for nothing. You can't be terrified of risk, because sometimes you have to be willing to go to the edge of your financial comfort zone in order to complete an investment or take your business to the next level.

Index